DA CAPO PRESS SERIES IN
ARCHITECTURE AND DECORATIVE ART
General Editor: ADOLF K. PLACZEK
Avery Librarian, Columbia University

14

The Works of
ASHER BENJAMIN

VI. The Builder's Guide

THE WORKS OF ASHER BENJAMIN

From the First Editions

Introduction by Everard M. Upjohn, *Columbia University*

THE BUILDER'S GUIDE

Illustrated By Sixty-six Engravings Which Exhibit
The Orders of Architecture And Other Elements Of
The Art

Designed For The Use of Builders, Particularly
of Carpenters And Joiners

BY ASHER BENJAMIN

DA CAPO PRESS · NEW YORK · 1974

Library of Congress Cataloging in Publication Data

Benjamin, Asher, 1773-1845.
    The builder's guide.

    (The works of Asher Benjamin, 6) (Da Capo Press
series in architecture and decorative art, 14)
    Reprint of the 1839 ed.
    1. Architecture — Orders.   2. Architecture —
Details.   I. Title.
NA2815.B4 1974   721   74-8676
ISBN 0-306-70971-6

This edition of *The Builder's Guide* is an
unabridged republication of the first edition
published in Boston and Philadelphia in 1839.

Published by Da Capo Press, Inc.
A Subsidiary of Plenum Publishing Corporation
227 West 17th Street
New York, New York 10011

Manufactured in the United States of America

THE
BUILDER'S GUIDE

THE

BUILDER'S GUIDE,

ILLUSTRATED BY

SIXTY-SIX ENGRAVINGS,

WHICH EXHIBIT THE ORDERS OF ARCHITECTURE

AND

OTHER ELEMENTS OF THE ART.

DESIGNED

FOR THE USE OF BUILDERS,

PARTICULARLY OF CARPENTERS AND JOINERS.

By ASHER BENJAMIN, Architect.

AUTHOR OF "THE AMERICAN BUILDER'S COMPANION," "THE RUDIMENTS OF ARCHITECTURE," "THE PRACTICAL
HOUSE CARPENTER," AND "PRACTICE OF ARCHITECTURE."

BOSTON:
PUBLISHED BY PERKINS & MARVIN.
PHILADELPHIA: HENRY PERKINS.
1839.

PREFACE.

————

THE present work, like the other works of the author, is designed principally for the use of those builders who reside at a distance from cities, where they cannot have the assistance of a regular architect. It is necessary for such, if they wish to excel in their occupation, to have a correct practical knowledge of architecture, and, for that purpose, to study such practical works as furnish the true principles of the art, and are adapted to their practice. No pains have been spared to give to this work the character which persons of this class will require. It contains all the elements and details of the art, from the most simple, to those the most difficult and complicated. Great labor has been bestowed upon the orders and their appendages, so as to render them intelligible, and in accordance with the practice of the day. The author has had regard to the habits and economy of this country, deviating, at the same time, as little as possible from the style and practice of Europe. He has made copious selections from many valuable works, for which he acknowledges a debt of gratitude; and he has also freely followed his own judgment and experience, in suggesting such alterations and ideas as appeared to him useful.

CONTENTS.

THE BUILDER'S GUIDE.

GRECIAN MOULDINGS.

Plate I.

THE outline of every Grecian moulding is taken from some one of the sections of the cone, and is susceptible, therefore, of as many variations as can be made of those sections. Different outlines are necessary in nearly all the great variety of situations in which these mouldings may be employed, and to ascertain the particular form best adapted to each situation, requires a discriminating eye, assisted by good practical judgment, and a knowledge of the effects produced on the surface of the mouldings by light and shade, by reflected light and surrounding objects. It would take so much time and labor to determine the particular section of the cone corresponding to the exact outline required in each case, as to forbid that course in common practice. I have therefore in my own practice, taken a thin mahogany veneer, and with a pen-knife and file cut it to the proper size and form of outline, judging by my eye ; and described the outline of the moulding by the pattern thus formed. If this practice be adopted, taking care to make new patterns when necessary, and never to alter old ones, it will not require a

2

great length of time to get possession of a sufficient number to answer for almost every case.

Fig. 1, D *b c d a e f g* A, is a section of the cone made by a plane passing through it parallel to one of its sides, and is called a parabola. D *b c d a e f g* A, on Fig. 2, represents a section of a cone made by a plane passing through perpendicular to its base, and is called a hyperbola. To draw Fig. 1, bisect D A and C B at *a* and *a*, and join *a a;* divide *a* A and *a* D, each into four equal parts and join; 1 *d,* 2 *c,* 3 *b* and 1 *e,* 2 *f,* 3 *g,* parallel to *a a;* divide D C and A B, each into four equal parts; from D C, draw lines 1 *a,* intersecting 3 *b* at *b,* and draw 2 *a* and 3 *a,* intersecting 2 *c* at *c,* and 1 *d* at *d;* from A B, draw 1 *a,* 2 *a,* and 3 *a,* intersecting 1 *e* at *e,* 2 *f* at *f,* and 3 *g* at *g;* then draw the curve line through the points D *b c d a e f g* A, which forms the section required.

The method of drawing the hyperbola differs from the above only in this, that the lines 1 *d,* 2 *c,* 3 *b,* and 1 *e,* 2 *f,* 3 *g,* would if produced, meet in a point at E.

C is drawn on the principle of the parabola, and D, on that of the hyperbola; C projects about one-half of Fig. 1, and D about one-half of Fig. 2. It will be seen, therefore, that a moulding of any height and projection may be drawn by this process, and that the only difference in drawing the examples E and F, is by inclining, in the latter case, the line on which the divisions are made, upwards, so that if produced, it would at no great distance from the moulding, intersect the line of the fillet, and that the more this line is inclined upward, the nearer the lower part of the moulding approaches to a straight line.

G is an example of a cymareversa, which is drawn on the principle of the parabola, and requires therefore nothing more than an examination of the Plate, to be understood.

To draw the cymarecta H, make *a d* its projection, and *d c* its height; bisect *a d* at *g,* and *b c* at *h,* and join *g h;* bisect *a b* at *e,* and *d c* at *f,* and

MOULDINGS

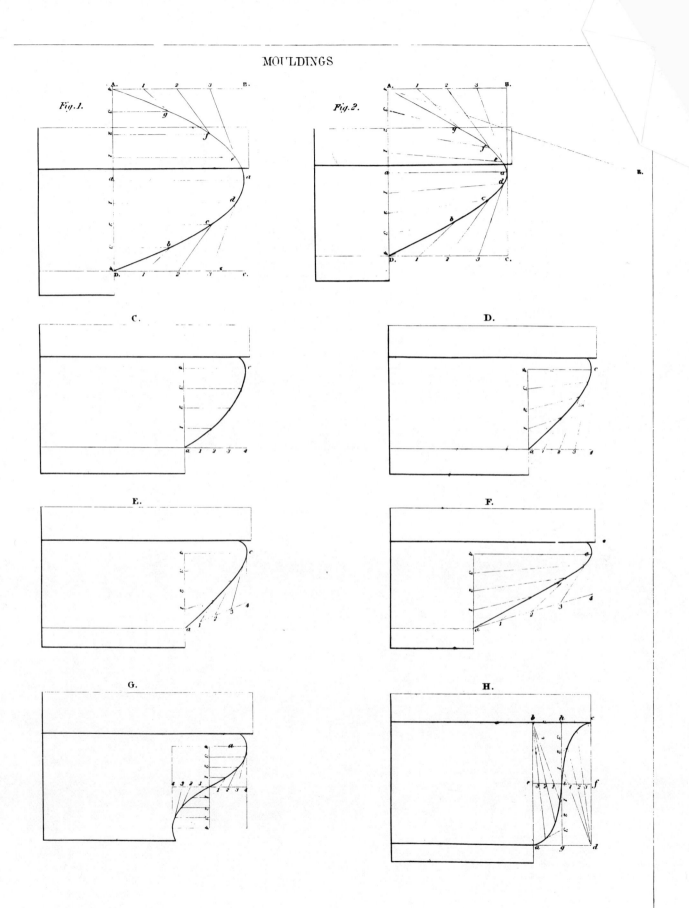

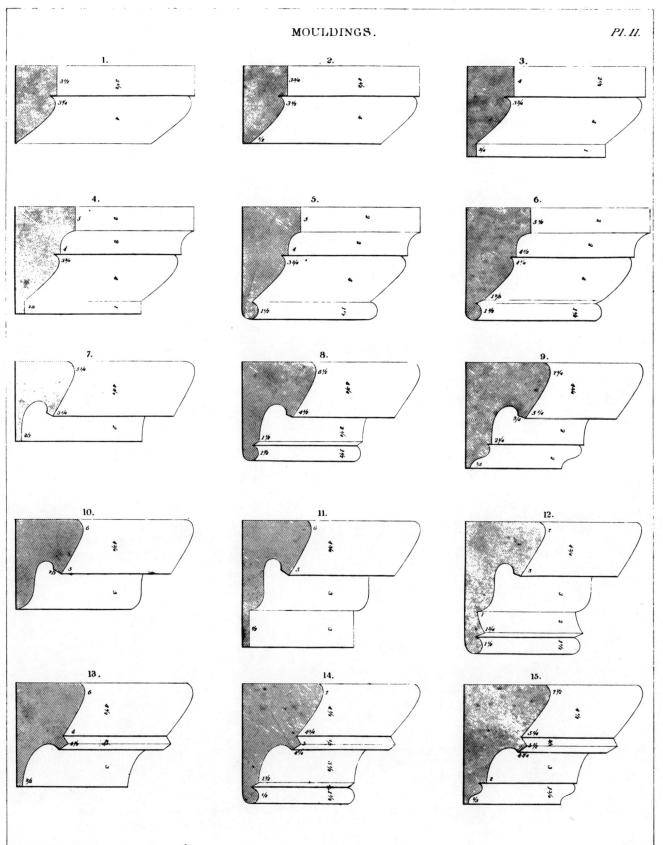

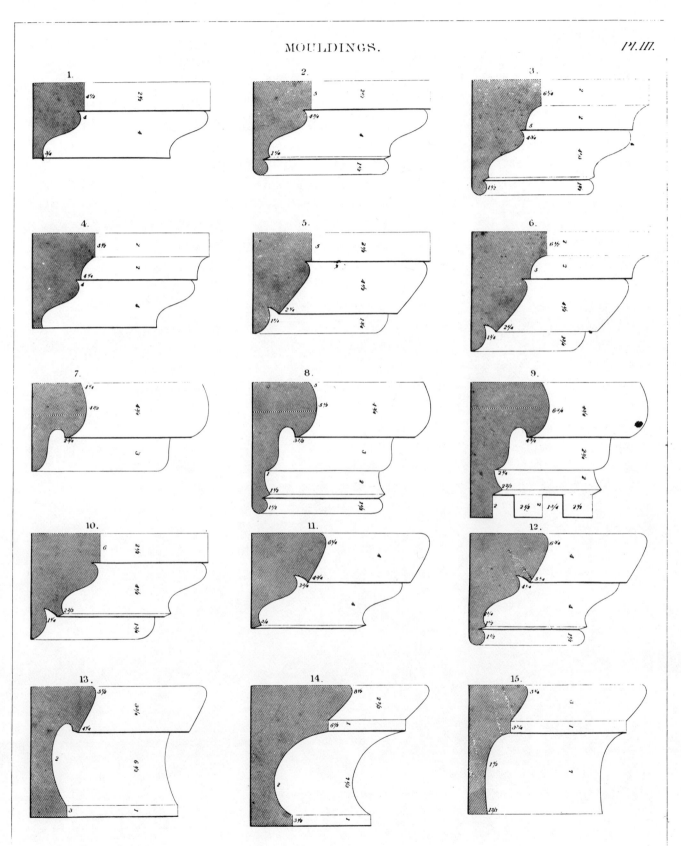

join *e f;* divide *i f*, *i e*, *i g*, and *i h*, each into a like number of equal parts, as in this instance into four ; from *d*, draw lines through the points 1 2 3 in *i f*, and continue them until they intersect other lines drawn from *c* to 1 2 3 on *i h*, and then, through these points of intersection, trace the curve of the moulding from *c* to *i*. Also from *b*, draw lines through the points 1 2 3 on *i e*, and continue them as before through the points 1 2 3 on *i g*, until they intersect other lines drawn from *a* to 1 2 3 on *i g;* then, through these points of intersection, draw the curve line of the moulding from *i* to *a*.

COMPOUND MOULDINGS.

Plates II. and III.

On these plates, are thirty different examples of sections for mouldings, all of which are drawn on a large scale, and figured for practice. They have been selected with great care, from the best Grecian examples ; but many of them are, in their form of outline and their particular combinations, entirely new ; and have not before, to my knowledge, appeared before the public in the form which they now assume. The practising carpenter will be able at once from these examples to select some one adapted to his purpose.

THE TUSCAN ORDER.

Plate IV.

Vitruvius has given this order a name, and assigned it a place with the other orders in his book, but he does not tell us of a single building on which it was employed. We are therefore left to suppose that its simple plainness did not suit the taste of the Romans of his day. It is said to have been invented by the inhabitants of Tuscany, before the Romans had intercourse with the Greeks, or had become acquainted with their arts and sciences. If this be true, we may presume that the eminent architects of those days did not consider it worthy of being employed on the public buildings erected by them, for if they had, some example of it would most certainly have been discovered among their ruins. The base of Trajan's column, and that of the third order of the Coliseum, are in imitation of the Tuscan base; but the capital of the latter is Corinthian, and the column is eight diameters and forty-seven minutes in height, and that of the former is Doric, and the column eight diameters in height. Neither of these examples can therefore be considered Tuscan.

Vitruvius is particular in explaining the proportions of the Tuscan temples. He gives the relative length, breadth and height of their walls, and also the number, size and distribution of the columns. He then describes the order, making the column seven diameters high, including base and capital, each of those members being one-half of a diameter in height. The column diminishes one-quarter of the lower diameter. The entablature is less than two diameters in height. It is difficult, however, to understand the exact height which it was intended the entablature should have. The frieze recedes a little from the face of the architrave, neither of which have either moulding or ornament. The cornice projects one fourth of the height of the column, which renders it unfit for common use. The modern architects who have written on the orders have, with trifling deviations, adopted this column as a standard, but the entablature has been rejected by them, each architect having composed an entablature as a substitute for that rejected, which he supposed better adapted to the column and to common use.

The following table exhibits the various members of the Tuscan order, by five distinguished architects, and it is singular to observe that no two of them have agreed in the height of the entablature or either of its members.

Pl. IV.

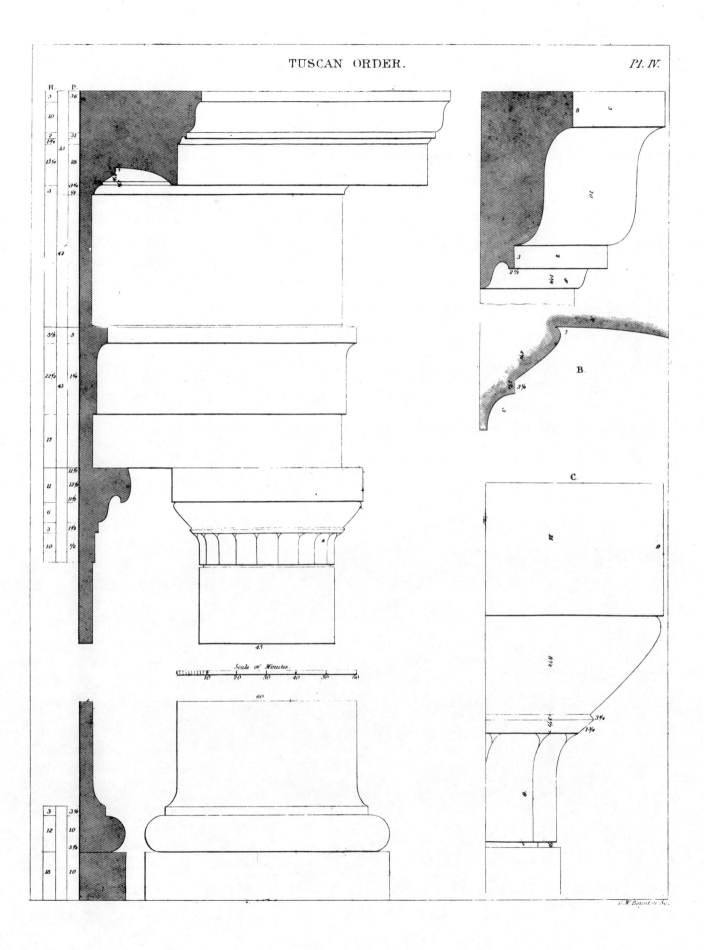

B.

C.

Scale of Minutes.

	Diameter in minutes.	Diameter at the back of the column.	Height of the column in diameters.	Height of entablature.	Height of architrave.	Height of freize.	Height of cornice.
Palladio, ...	60.	45.	7.	1.44½	35	26	43½
Scamozi, ...	60.	45.	7.30	1.52½	32½	39	41
Serlio, ...	60.	45.	6.	1.30	30	30	30
Vignola, ...	60.	48.	7.	1.40	25	35	40
Sir William Chambers, ...	60.	50.	7.	1.45	31½	31½	42
Sum total, ...		233.	34.30	7.12	154	162	197
Average, ...		46½	6.54	1.42½	31	32½	39½

A perfect fitness, harmony and proportion must exist between the column, its entablature, and the several members of the latter, or the composition is defective ; and as an explanation of the reasons which induce us to believe that the above entablatures are not of a sufficient height to produce that effect, we will consider the entablature in the relation of a beam of sufficient size, or apparently so, to sustain a weight equal to that of the columns on which each end of the beam rests. It is well known that, the greater the distance the columns or supports to the beam are from each other, the larger must be the bulk of the beam, to answer its intended purpose. Vitruvius, and the respectable authors above named, have placed the Tuscan columns at a greater distance from each other, than those of either of the other orders. It follows therefore, that, to preserve symmetry and proportion, this entablature must be made at least equal in height to those of the other orders ; and it has therefore received in this example the same relative height to the column. But it is not supposed that the height, here allowed to either the column or its entablature, will at all times and places be the one most suitable. For example, a column which has apparently but a small burthen to support does not require to be made so large, as one which has to sustain a very great weight. Nor does an entablature, whose length does not exceed ten or twenty feet, require to be made so high, as one which stretches unbroken through the whole length of a large building, from seventy to one hundred feet.

As diameters and minutes are the standard measures by which this and the other orders are drawn, it may be well to explain what these measures are.

A diameter, is the distance across the shaft of the column at its base, whether large or small; and a minute, is one-sixtieth part of a diameter. The height and projection of all the different members of the order are figured in minutes.

The column of figures under H, expresses the heights of the members, and those under P, their projections.

Suppose it be required to draw this order to a height of seventeen feet, four inches; now, because the column is seven diameters, and the entablature two, which added together make nine, we divide the seventeen feet, four inches, into nine equal parts, one of which will be twenty-three and one-ninth inches, and is equal to the diameter of the column. Subdivide this into sixty equal parts, as shown by the scale of minutes on the Plate.

A, shows a section of the crown moulding; B, a section of the bed mould; C, a profile of the capital, drawn on a large scale, for the purpose of showing in the clearest manner the particular form of these mouldings.

COLUMN AND ENTABLATURE.

PLATE V.

The example here given of a column and entablature, will be found useful, when the Tuscan order is thought to be too plain, and the Doric too expensive. The shaft of the column is divided into sixteen flutes, in imitation of its

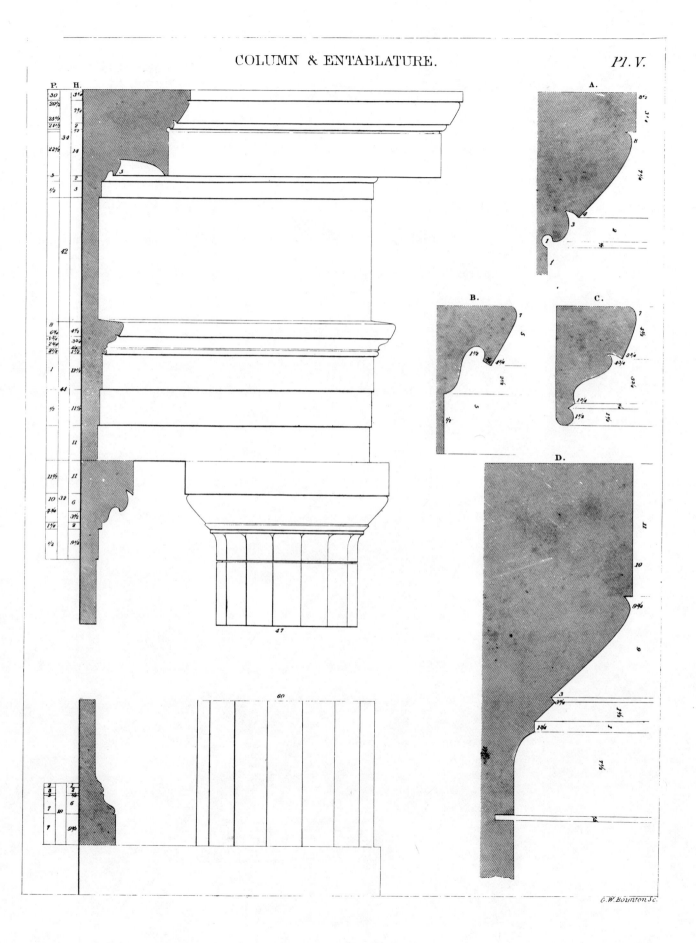

A.

B.

C.

D.

original, which is taken from the temple at Sunium. This is the only example of all the Grecian antiquities which had less than twenty flutes. Where the column is of very large dimensions, it will have a bold and impressive effect; but when the column does not exceed eight or ten inches in diameter, and extends eight or more diameters in height, it has the appearance of being about to make an indentation into the step on which it stands, an effect which will be relieved by adding a base. The several members of this entablature have been selected from such of the Grecian examples, as were supposed most suitable. This column may be made seven or eight or more diameters in height, as circumstances may require. The entablature is two diameters in height.

A, exhibits a section of the crown moulding of the cornice; B, a section of the bed mould; C, a section of the band of the architrave; and D, a section of the capital, all of which are drawn on a large scale for the purpose of showing the outline of the mouldings. A section of the capital of the antae is shown in No. 2, Plate XVI., and of the base at C, Plate XX.

DORIC ORDER.

Plate VI.

This order, together with the Ionic and Corinthian, is of Greek invention. Enough of those renowned temples, which were built by the Greeks after these orders, have withstood the ravages of time and the rapacity of barbarians, to make manifest the skill and splendid talents of their architects. We are indebted, first to Stewart and Revel, and then to several distinguished English architects, for very accurate measurements and delineations of these temples, with all their details, and also for many fragments of other buildings. We are not therefore obliged to depend upon any vague and doubtful representations, in relation to the inventions and practice of these orders, as in the case of the Tuscan order.

The Doric order was invented for some time and employed on many buildings, before the invention of either of the others. It has graceful forms and massive proportions. Its columns varied very much in their proportions in different buildings. In the early practice of the order, the column appears to have been made only four diameters and four minutes in height, but at later periods the Grecian architects increased its height to six diameters and thirty-two minutes. The height of the entablature also, and the proportions of its different members varied very considerably. No two examples, which were erected at about the same time and by the same architect, agree either in the height of their columns, or of the entablature, or in their details. The Grecian architects, it seems, looked first at the object to be effected, and then gave the requisite proportions to the different parts of the building. They nevertheless contrived, with all their deviations in practice, to retain the severe Doric character, by uniformly resting the column on a step or floor without base moulding, by fluting the shaft with twenty broad flat flutes without intervening fillets, making from three to five annulets on the capital, and by the triglyphs and metopes in the frieze, and the mutules in the cornice; none of which details were ever omitted, let the other deviations be ever so great. In some very fine specimens of this order, the necking and a space at the base of about equal height were fluted, leaving the remaining part of the shaft plain. The massive simplicity of the Grecian Doric, produced by a skillful arrangement of its details, will be sought for in vain in the Roman Doric, with its slender column and details badly adapted and arranged.

We have made no attempt to assign a determinate height to the column of the example here given, as it will be necessary to adapt its height to the situation in which it shall be placed. With a view to assist the judgment of the student in deciding upon the proper proportions of columns, we have given

DORIC ORDER.

Pl. VI.

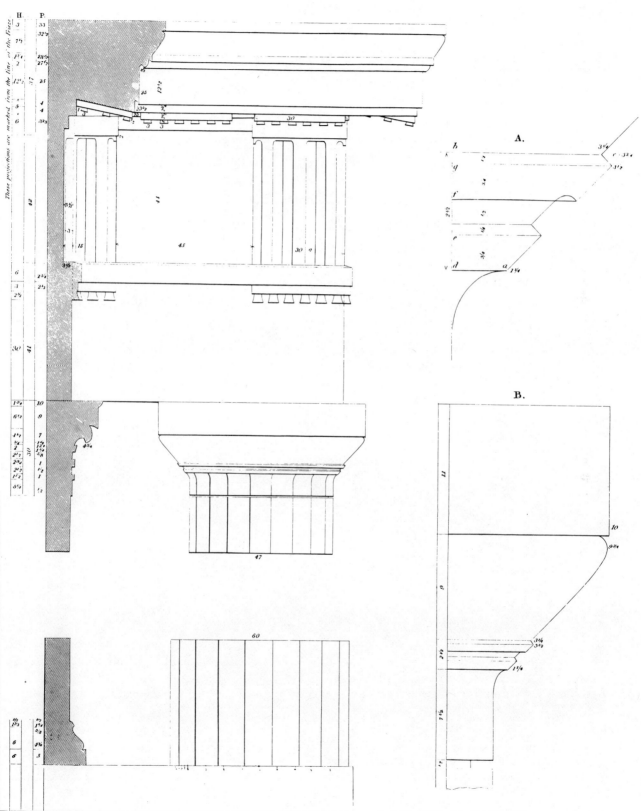

A.

B.

J. W. Boynton Sc.

below some of the extremes of the practice of the Grecian and Roman architects.

The Temple at Corinth, ...	4 diameters,		4 minutes.	
The Temple of Jupiter at Selinus, . . .	4 "		34 "	
The Temple of Minerva at Athens, . . .	5 "		33 "	
The Temple of Theseus, ...	5 "		42 "	
The Temple of Propylea, ...	5 "		54 "	
The Temple of Apollo, ...	6 "		3 "	
The Portico of Phillip, ...	6 "		32 "	
The Temple of Jupiter Nemeus, ...	6 "		31 "	
The Theatre of Marcellus at Rome, . . .	7 "		51 "	
The Theatre of Albano near Rome, . . .	7 "			
Vitruvius, ...	7 "			
Palladio, ...	8 "			
Scamozzi, ...	8 "			
Vignola, ...	8 "			

The three last mentioned authors have added a base to the column, which reduces the shaft thirty minutes in height.

It will be seen from the above list that the Grecian architects varied the proportion of their columns from four diameters and four minutes, to six diameters thirty-two minutes; a difference of two diameters and thirty-two minutes; but this is a greater variation than it will be necessary for us to use in our practice. It is supposed that the Doric column will not require a height of less than six, nor more than seven diameters in any situation. It requires however more consideration to determine their height than it does those of the other orders, because the centre of a triglyph must be placed over the centre of each column, with the exception of those triglyphs which form the angles of the frieze, so that the intercolumniation next to the angular columns will be something less than that of the others. The intercolumniation will be one and a half diameters, where only one triglyph is placed over it; and two and three quarters diameters where two are placed over it. To determine the diameter and height of the columns of a Grecian portico,

4

suppose (No. 2, Plate XXI.) the front to have four columns and to extend twenty-four feet nine inches, divide that distance into thirty-three equal parts, each of which will be nine inches, give four of these parts which will be three feet to the diameter of the column. Make the centre intercolumniation equal to one and a half diameters of the column, or four feet six inches, and make each of those intercolumniations next to the angular columns, four feet one and one-half inches. Now suppose the column to be six diameters and the entablature two diameters in height .he portico will then be twenty-four feet in height. Suppose the facade to be extended to thirty-nine feet, nine inches, so as to make a portico of six columns in front, (see No. 1,) divide the front line into fifty-three equal parts, each of which will be nine inches, and four of these will be three feet, or equa' .o the diameter of the column, the intercolumniation will be the same as in the last example, and if the column is six diameters high, the whole height of the portico will also be the same as before.

It will be seen that neither of these examples, although beautiful in themselves, can be employed on dwelling-houses of two stories in height, because the entablature would in that case extend from the eaves downward a distance of six feet or more, and would of course cover and destroy the second story windows. If the columns to the last example were made seven diameters high, the height of the building would be twenty-seven feet, and sufficient for a church where a gallery is not wanted; and as the intercolumniation is small, a harmonious effect would be thereby produced.

From what has been said it appears that the Greeks first determined the extent of the front line of their temples, and then made the diameter of the column a certain portion of that line, and that the height of the building depended on that of the column and en tature. It will be wise to remember these facts, and never suffer ourselves to deviate much from the same method.

Plate VII.

On this Plate is a section of the Doric cornice, with its plancere inverted; also a section and front elevation of the triglyph, showing its peculiar connection with the bed mould. These details have been carefully drawn on a large scale, and figured in minutes for the purpose of giving the student a clear and distinct knowledge of this complicated entablature, which is at least three times in four imperfectly drawn and put together when not done by an architect.

On Plate XII., No. 4, is exhibited a plan and elevation of the drop at the lower extremity of the triglyph, accurately drawn and figured in minutes, and at No. 3, on the same Plate, a section of the Doric flutes. To draw the latter, divide $d\,5$ into four equal parts, and with the distance $d\,5$ on d and 5, make the intersection b from b, and through the points 1 and 4, draw lines to c and e, divide $b\,c$ and $b\,e$, each into five equal parts; on $b\,c$ at a, and $b\,e$ at a, with the distance $a\,d$ or $a\,5$, describe the curved lines $d\,c$, and $5\,e$, and lastly with the distance $b\,c$ or $b\,e$, describe the curve $c\,e$. This method of forming the flutes by parts of a circle is not recommended as the best for that purpose, but may be used to ascertain their depth, and then it will be best to form the section of the flutes from the ellipsis.

IONIC ORDER.

Plate VIII.

This was the second, in point of time, of the Grecian orders. The column was generally made eight diameters in height, always standing upon a base composed of a series of mouldings, which differ in number and form in different examples. The shaft diminished about ten minutes, and was decorated with twenty-four flutes, having either a semi-circular or semi-elliptical section, and separated by fillets of about one-fourth of their breadth. The capital always maintains the same character, but in form and richness of ornament, it varied very much in different examples. The capitals of the Erectheum were very highly ornamented and very beautiful, but the great number of spiral lines winding round the eye of the volutes, render this example less pleasing when employed upon small than it is upon large columns. Those which adorned the columns of the little temple situated on the banks of the river Ilissus, possessed a fitness, a classical beauty and harmonious combination of parts in which they are universally allowed to excel all others. Great deviations are found in the different examples of the entablature, in their height, form, and the number and richness of their mouldings. Its relative height to that of the column cannot now be determined, as the upper extremity of the cornices, consisting generally of the crown moulding, is wanting; but judging from the height of the architrave, the frieze and the remaining part of the cornice, that of the entablature must have generally been two diameters.

The example here given is not in exact imitation of any one of the Grecian Ionics, but is in all respects purely Grecian. In selecting its various members from ancient examples, it has been our aim to adapt it to the wants and practice of the present day.

The column was made by the Grecians from eight to nine diameters in height, which rule has been followed by the Romans and the moderns, and we cannot do better than to imitate them. The height of the entablature in this example is two diameters.

Plate IX.

This Plate contains a second and more ornamented example of the Ionic order. Its general proportions are intended to be the same as those of the first example. The beautiful ornaments upon the neck of the capital are

IONIC ORDER.

Pl. VIII.

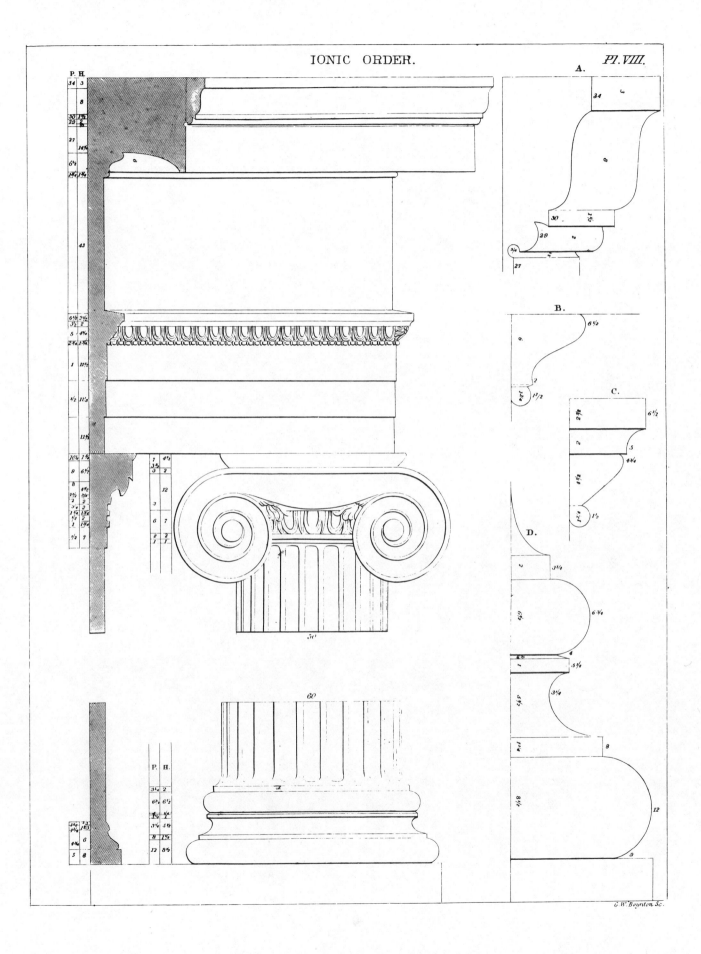

G.W. Boynton Sc.

Pl. IX.

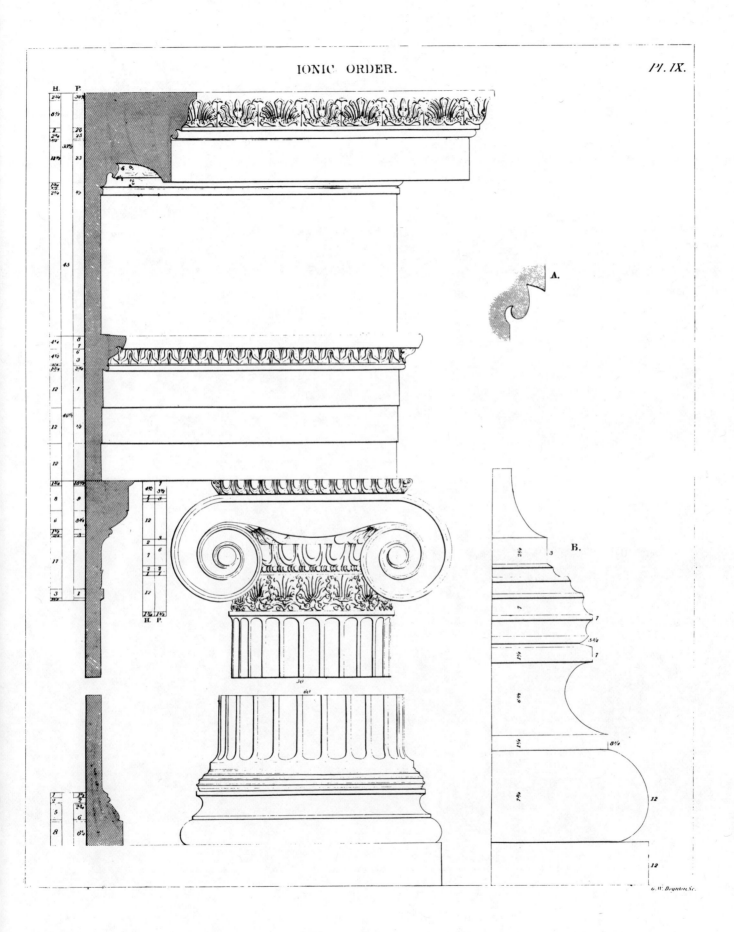

taken from the Erechtheus at Athens, and the leaves upon the bolster part, from a fine specimen of this capital discovered near the wall of the Acropolis at Athens.

For the sake of variety, in the base, the upper torus is fluted, in imitation of some very fine Grecian examples of the Ionic base. The fluted base, though its profile appears beautiful, when represented on paper, does not, when executed, possess that chaste beauty which is presented by the plain ones.

Plate X.

On this Plate are the details of the Ionic capital, carefully drawn on a large scale, and figured for practice.

The carver will find it to his advantage to imitate these drawings faithfully, and thus escape the censure deservedly cast upon the many clumsy, awkward productions of this capital, which may be seen in both town and country.

No. 1, exhibits a front elevation of one-half of the capital; and No. 2, a section through, from a to b, on No. 1. No. 4, represents a section of one-fourth part of the column and an inverted view of one-fourth part of the capital. No. 3, on this Plate, shows a section from a to b, on the side elevation of the capital, which is exhibited at No. 1, Plate XII.

To draw the volute No. 1. At two minutes distance from the shaft of the column, draw the vertical line b a; on o* as a centre, which is twenty minutes distant from the underside of the abacus at a, describe the eye, making it seven minutes in diameter; at the distance of one and one-fourth of a minute above and below the centre of the eye, draw lines at right angles with b a, and at the distance of one and one-half minutes from b a, and parallel therewith, draw the line 10, 11, which completes the outline of the square. From the point o, draw the diagonals o 10, and o 11, and divide each of them into three equal parts; from these points, and at right angles with b a, draw lines cutting b a at 1, 5, and 4, 8. The points numbered from 1 to 11, are the

* See the eye of the volute at A, drawn on a large scale.

5

centres, on which the volute is drawn. The twelfth centre is found, by continuing the line at the top of the square, one and a half minutes across $b\,a$ to 12. On 1, as a centre, and with the distance $1\,c$, draw $c\,d$; on 2, and with the distance $2\,d$, draw $d\,e$; on 3, and with the distance $3\,e$, draw $e\,f$; with the distance $4\,f$, draw $f\,g$, which completes one revolution. On 5, draw $g\,h$; on 6, draw $h\,i$; on 7, draw $i\,j$; on 8, draw $j\,k$; on 9, draw $k\,l$; on 10, draw $l\,m$; on 11, draw $m\,n$; and on 12, draw $n\,p$, which completes the outline of the volute. To draw the inside line, divide the fillet into twelve equal parts, and make the fillet at n, equal to eleven of these parts, and that at m, equal to ten of the same parts, and so on, diminishing its width one-twelfth at each quarter of a revolution. It will however be best to lessen this diminution at each quarter, after passing about one and one-half revolutions, or the fillet will, before its termination, appear too small. It is intended that the face of the architrave shall be placed vertically over the line $b\,a$, which is two minutes distant from the side of the column at its neck.

Plate XI.

On this Plate, the details of the capital of the second example of the Ionic order are drawn on a large scale and figured for practice.

THE CORINTHIAN ORDER.

Plate XIII.

This order is the third and last in point of time, of the Grecian orders. It does not appear to have been so much a favorite with the Greeks, as to have been employed by them very frequently on their public buildings: and how often it was used on their private buildings we cannot now determine, as none of those have withstood the ravages of time. Stuart and Revet have

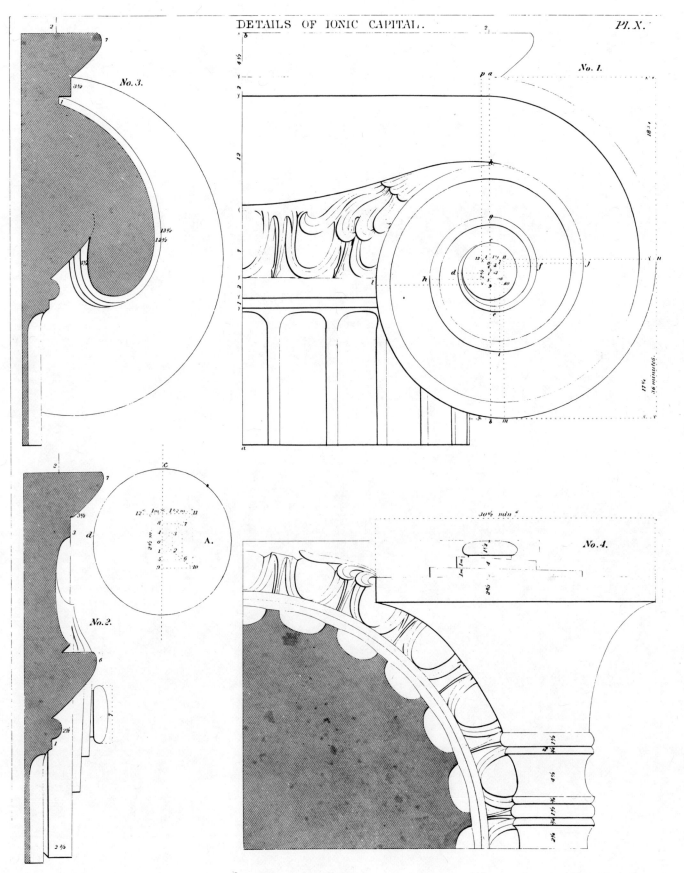

No. 3.

No. 1.

No. 2.

A.

No. 4.

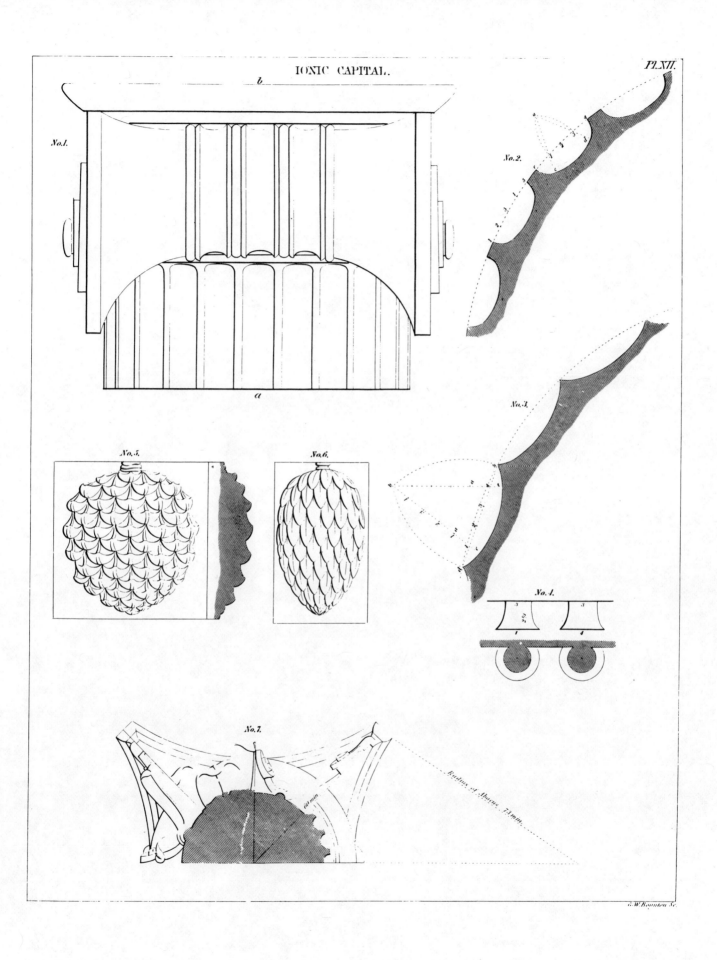

IONIC CAPITAL.

PL. XII.

No. 1.

No. 2.

No. 3.

No. 5.

No. 6.

No. 4.

No. 7.

G. W. Boynton Sc.

measured and published several fine examples of this order, some of which are supposed to have been erected while the Romans held dominion over Greece.

Several of the entablatures do not appear to have been formed with the same taste and judgment which is displayed upon the columns, bases and capitals, which the Greeks so universally exercised in the other orders.

The Romans adopted this order from the Greeks, and it at once became a favorite with them, which they employed in almost all their public buildings. In their hands it underwent many important changes. They added a modillion to the cornice, of a very rich character, and other new members to the bed mould, and their architects appear to have vied with each other in embellishing the mouldings, and many of the flat surfaces of the entablature, with costly and beautiful sculpture.

The column and capital of this example do not materially differ from those of the Grecian and Roman examples; but in the entablature, an intermediate course has been adopted, it being somewhat more embellished than the Grecian, and much less so than the Roman.

The addition of the modillion and other new members to the bed mould, by the Romans, made its height about two-thirds of the whole height of the cornice. Sir William Chambers very properly makes three divisions of a cornice, viz: the corona, which predominates and is principal in the composition, the bed mould, whose office is to support and give stability to the corona, and the crown mouldings, which serve to shelter and protect the corona from falling water and other falling bodies. It appears, therefore, that the bed mould ought not to occupy so much space, as the Roman architects gave to it. In imitation of the Grecian practice, the modillion has not been added to this cornice. It is proposed to make the column, including base and capital, ten diameters, and the entablature, two and three-quarters diameters, in height.

Plate XIV.

A second example of the Corinthian order, from the Choragic monument of Lysicrates at Athens. In this example, such deviations from the original have been made, as it was thought were required, in order to give it a more particular adaptation to our practice. It is proposed to make the column, including the base and capital, ten diameters, and the entablature, two and a quarter diameters, in height.

The channel which encircles the neck of the column, and the leaves which divide it from the capital, in the original, are omitted in this example, because they appear to have been taken from the neck of the Doric column, which is decorated with the same channel, the flutes of the shaft passing up through it and terminating under the annulus of the capital. The original of this capital is supposed to be the most ancient of the order, and is unlike that of any other example which has been as yet discovered. Its classic expression and admirable adaptation to the place which it occupies, have rendered it a favorite with all lovers of architecture. It will be found that I have not followed the entablature of the original in every particular, especially in the details of the cornice, some of the mouldings of which have received a different size and form of outline, but the general character and expression have been faithfully preserved.

A section of the abacus is drawn at large and figured in minutes on Plate III., No. 14.

Plate XV.

A third example of the Corinthian order. This capital is said to have been discovered among the fragments of the temple of Apollo, at Branchidæ, near Miletus. The fragment, though much defaced when found, retained enough of its original appearance, to enable the moderns to make out all its details, except the abacus. The graceful simplicity of its form, the care, with which

Pl. XIV.

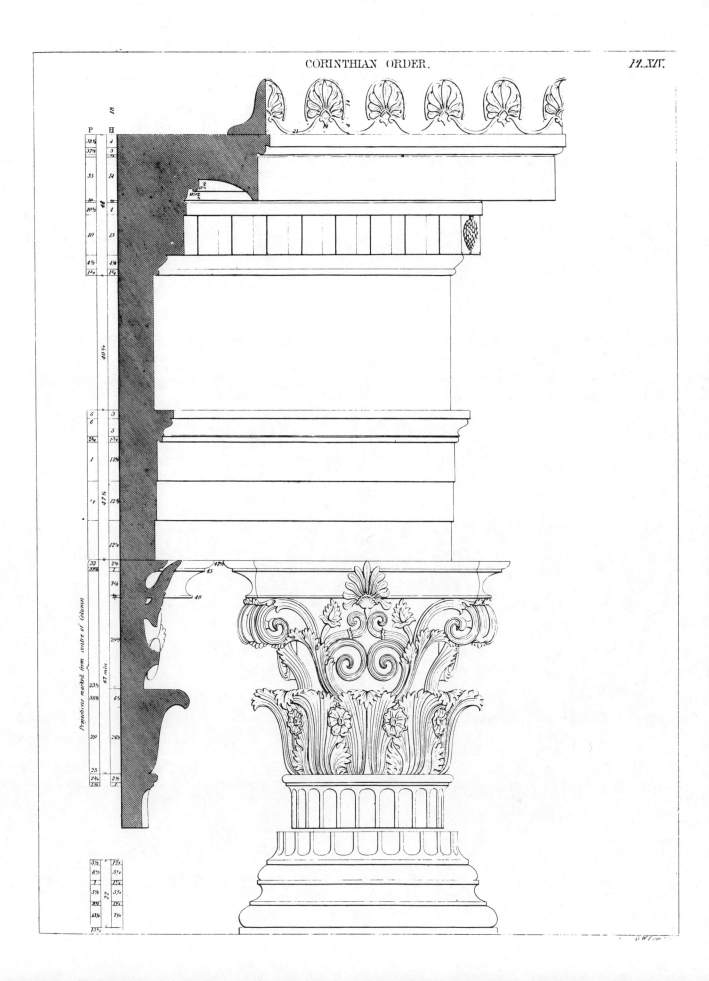

it may be wrought, and its adaptation to many situations which come within our practice, have induced me to add to it a column and entablature, and recommend it for imitation, though I am not aware that it has been used upon any buildings, ancient or modern, except the temple above mentioned. The general proportions of the column and entablature are the same as those of the two preceding examples. A section of the abacus is drawn at large on Plate III., No. 13, and figured in minutes.

PLATE XVI.

On this Plate are six different designs for antae capitals. No. 1, is intended for the antae to the Tuscan order; No. 2, for the antae exhibited on Plate V.; No. 3, for that of the Doric order; and Nos. 4, 5, and 6, for those of the Ionic and Corinthian orders. The outlines of these capitals are drawn on a large scale and figured in minutes.

It is not intended to confine their use within the limits mentioned above; they may be used with success wherever their peculiar form and character harmonize with the other parts of the composition.

PLATE XVII.

On this Plate are three designs for antae capitals, differing in form and richness of character from those on the preceding Plate. The embellishments of No. 1, are remarkably chaste and elegant. They are taken from a Grecian fragment. They are of great value to the carpenter who is situated at a distance from a carver, inasmuch as they can be wrought by himself. The neck of No. 2, is taken from that of the second example of the Ionic order, and is therefore to be used always on the antae accompanying that order; it may also be used in any other situation, where its character will harmonize with that of the surrounding objects. No. 3, is also of a rich

6

character, and is better adapted to inside than to outside finishing, but may be used with propriety in either case. The outlines of the details of these capitals are drawn on a large scale and figured in minutes.

Plate XVIII.

On this Plate is given an example of the antae and entablature, copied, with deviations, from that on the choragic monument of Thrasyllus at Athens. Their details are in themselves beautiful, and are arranged with such judgment and good taste, as to give a simple elegance to the whole composition. The deviations from the original are not very great; they are in the bed mould, architrave and capital, and in adding a base to the antae.

A, shows a section of the crown moulding; B, a section of the bed mould; and C, a section of the base to the antae, all drawn on a large scale, for the purpose of exhibing the outline of those mouldings. This example may be drawn by diameters and minutes, like the orders, and the antae be made about eight diameters in height.

Plate XIX.

This example of an antae and entablature is, in character and effect, Doric, having mutules in the cornice, which are so arranged, as to permit the space between them to be decorated with rosettes. The architrave bears a strong resemblance to that of the choragic monument of Thrasyllus at Athens, but the outlines of its details are quite different from that example. The capital is, in character and effect, Doric, though it differs in its outline from that of any other example of that order. The crown moulding of the cornice is singular in the form of its outline. It is so constructed as to cause a strong shade to be thrown upon its lower surface, which relieves it from the corona. The mutule is in size and form like that shown on Plate VII.

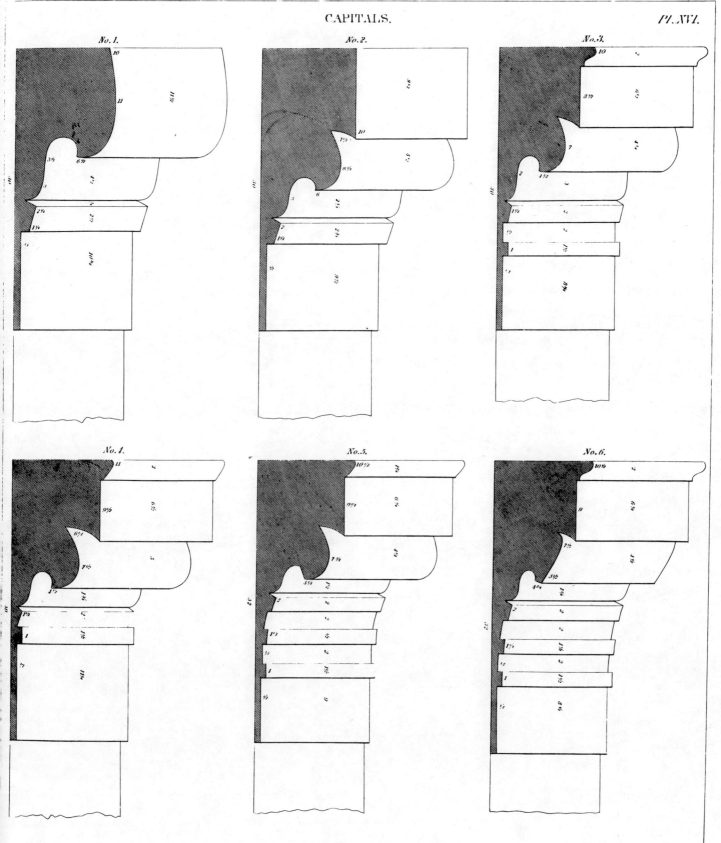

No. 1.   No. 2.   No. 3.

No. 4.   No. 5.   No. 6.

No. 1

No. 2

No. 3

G. W. Boynton Sc.

Pl. XVIII.

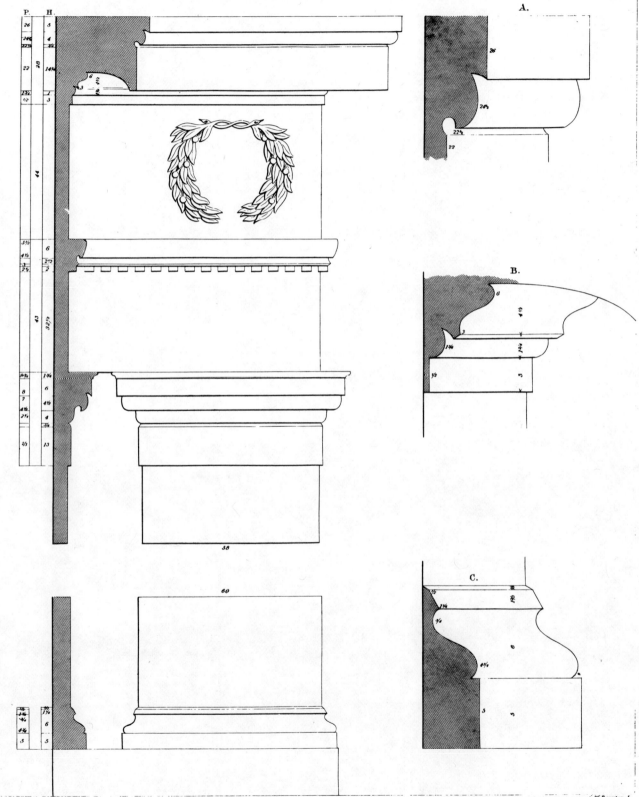

A.

B.

C.

G. W. Boynton S.

Pl. XIX.

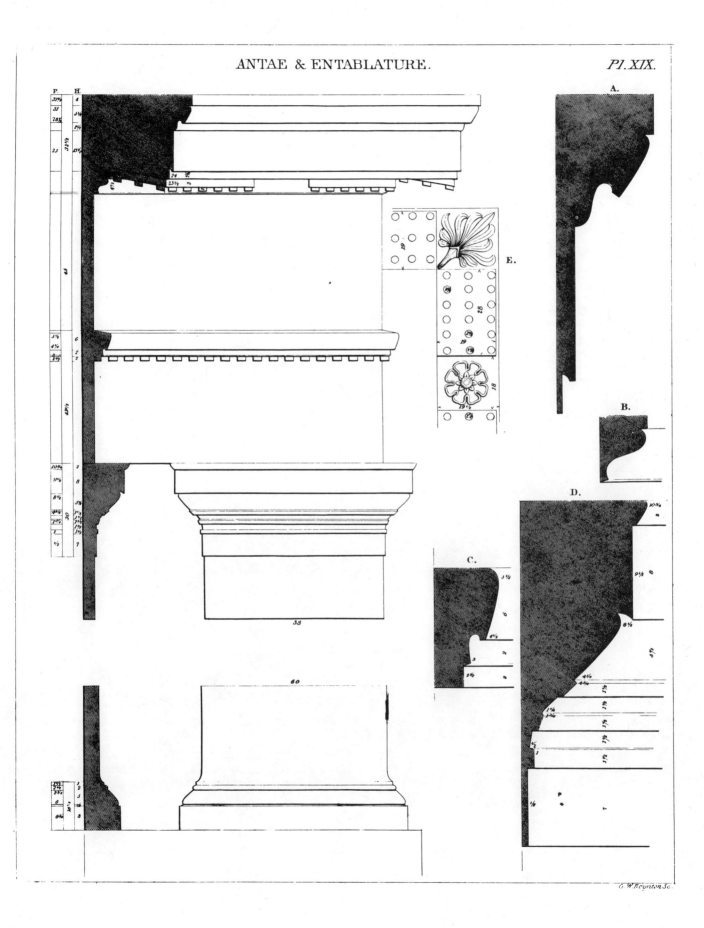

A.

E.

B.

D.

C.

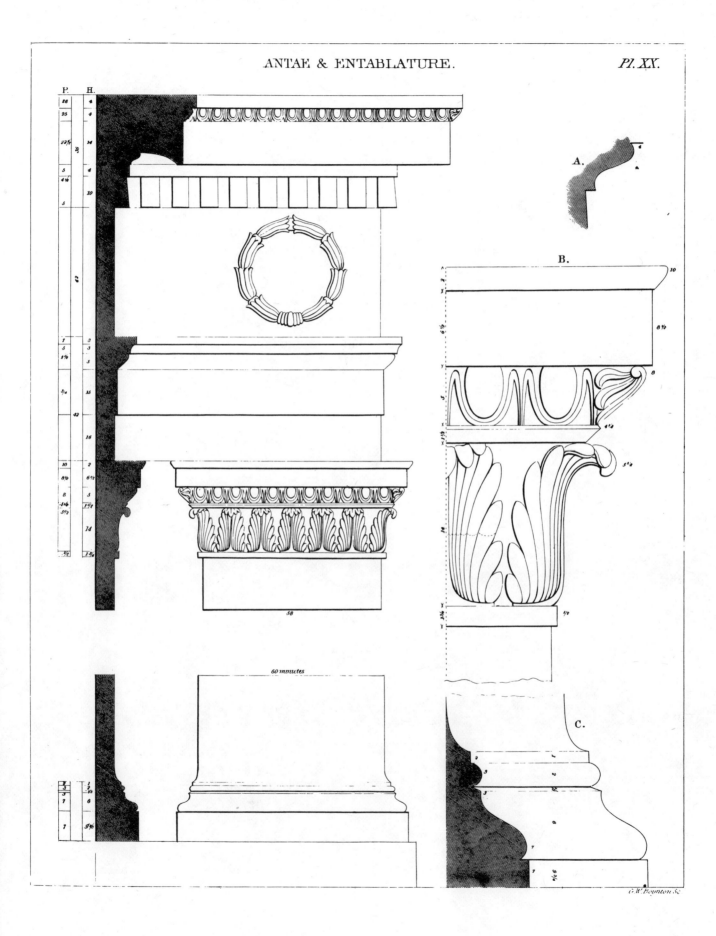

60 minutes

A.

B.

C.

A, shows a section of the crown moulding and corona; B, a section of the bed mould; C, one of the architraves; D, a section of the capital figured-in minutes; and F, shows the plancere inverted.

Plate XX.

The details of this example of an antae and entablature are of a more delicate character than those of the preceding one; and it is therefore more particularly adapted to inside than to outside finishing, though it may be used with success in either. The elements of this example are few and simple, and will produce a pleasing effect, if the situation in which it is to be used is selected with judgment. The wreath, which adorns the frieze, is taken from an example in Stuart's Antiquities of Athens. This and the capitals of the antae partake of the same simple character, and both may be wrought with the greatest ease by an intelligent carpenter, if necessary, without the aid of a carver. The distance between the several wreaths may be about equal to the width of the frieze.

A, shows a section of the bed mould; B, a profile of the capital; and C, a profile of the base moulding; all of which are figured in minutes.

INTERCOLUMNIATIONS.

Plate XXI.

Plate XXI. exhibits an elevation of a Doric portico, with six columns in front, and also plans of other examples, of which Nos. 1 and 2, have been explained in the description of the Doric order. The necessity is there shown of a systematic and harmonious distribution of the columns and the details of the entablature. No. 3, exhibits a plan of a portico, with four columns, whose extent is thirty-six feet.   This extent is divided into forty-eight equal parts, each part being equal to nine inches, and four of these parts, or three feet, are equal to the diameter of the column, eleven, to the centre intercolumniation, and ten and one-half, to each of the other two.   These intercolumniations require that two triglyphs should be placed over each.   No. 4, shows a plan of four columns, extending twenty-eight feet, six inches.   That extent is divided into thirty-eight equal parts, and the column made equal to four of these parts, the centre intercolumniation, to eleven, and each of the other two, to five and one-half parts. Two triglyphs must be placed over the centre intercolumniation, and one, over each of the other two.

In common practice, when the columns are much less than three feet in diameter, they cannot generally be placed nearer to each other than those of No. 3, because the interval between them would in that case be insufficient to enable a person of large size to pass between them freely. Take for instance the example of a piazza to be erected in front of a dwelling-house, whose columns are one foot six inches in diameter.   In that case, the distance between the columns, if set in imitation of No. 1 or 2, would be only two feet three inches, which would be about one-half of the breadth of the windows of the house: and if they were set in imitation of No. 3, the distance would be four feet one and a half inches, which also would be insufficient.   It would be expedient therefore, in such a case, to place three triglyphs over each intercolumniation.   It is however to be observed, that when the intercolumniation is so extended as to admit three triglyphs over it, it produces a lean and unsolid aspect, by reason of the numerous and massive details of the entablature, which require the appearance of frequent support.   Hence the student will perceive that this order succeeds better, when wrought on a large than on a small scale, and it will be well for him, in cases like the above, to use one of the other orders, in which the same nicety is not required in placing the columns, as will be perceived by the following description.

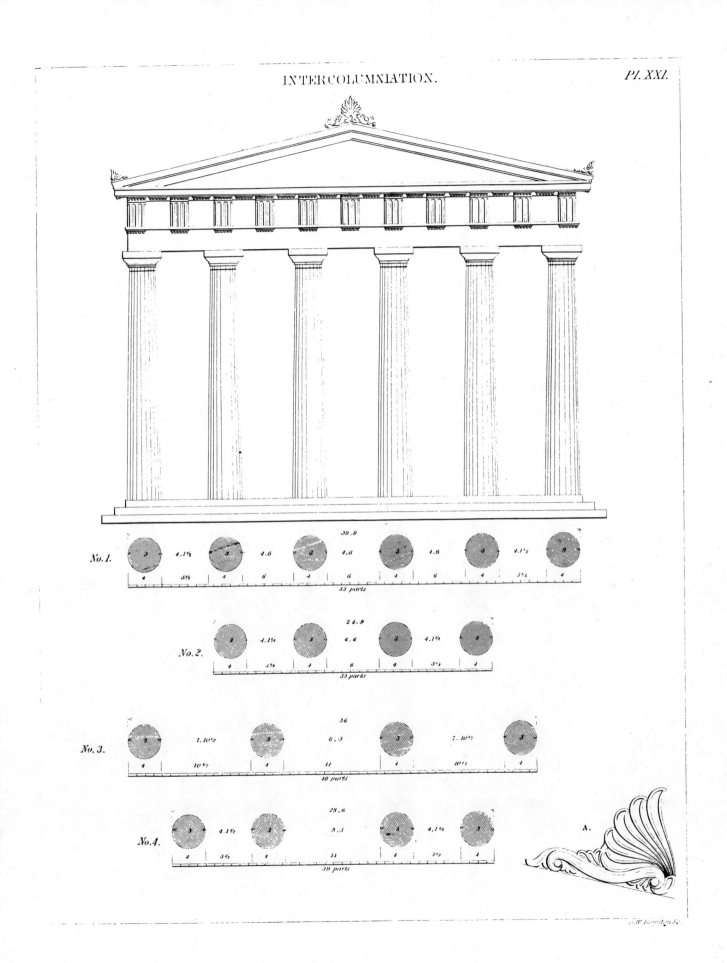

No. 1.

No. 2.

No. 3.

No. 4.

A.

Vitruvius describes the different intercolumniations by the following names, which are still preserved by modern architects. Pycnostylos, when the distance between the columns is once and one-half their diameter; Systylos, when it is two diameters; Eustylos, when it is two and one-quarter diameters; Diostylos, when it is three diameters; Araeostylos, when it is four diameters.

The wide range here given for the placing of columns will admonish the student to be circumspect, in making his selection, that the intercolumniation may harmonize with the form and style of the object with which it is connected.

PEDESTALS.

PLATE XXII.

The use of pedestals appears to have been an innovation in the Grecian practice, and was introduced into that country subsequently to the loss of its political independence. In the original examples we find the columns standing upon the uppermost of three steps, a rule, to which the temple of Theseus at Athens is believed to furnish the only exception.

The Romans, on the other hand, raised the floors of their temples to the height of the pedestal, projecting it forward, so that the steps in front, by which the temple was entered, profiled against it. In the ancient theatres, the inferior orders rested on steps, while the superior orders stood on pedestals, which formed a parapet, and raised the base of the order sufficiently high to be seen on a near approach to the building, and for the spectators to lean over.

Since the Grecian style of architecture has, at the present day, universally prevailed over the Roman, pedestals are not held in very high estimation.

But though they cannot be considered as a necessary appendage to any of the orders, they are nevertheless so often used with them, as to require some notice, as to their proportions and their fitness for different situations.

Pedestals sometimes supply the place of a basement. They are also used for supporting colonades, ballustrades, attics, &c. Sir William Chambers makes their height equal to three-tenths of the height of the column sustained by them. This rule will generally be found correct; but cases may occur in practice, when different proportions will be required, in which event all the peculiar circumstances of the case must be regarded, and the proportions of the pedestal so modified, as to accord with the architectural objects connected with it. Pedestals should never be insulated, though the column supported by them be so; and the dye should never be less than the diameter of the base of the column. When they are employed in balustrades, the dye, should be equal to the neck of the column, or antae, over which they stand.

On Plate XXII. are exhibited base mouldings and cornices for the Tuscan, Doric and Ionic orders, all of which are figured in minutes, the length of the scale being equal to the diameter of the column.

PLATE XXIII.

On Plate XXIII., at C, is exhibited a pedestal which has a base and cornice extending along and forming a part of a ballustrade, showing the balusters in their proper position and distance from each other, commencing with one-half of one baluster, against the edge of the pedestal. The pedestal is supposed to stand at the eaves of the building and directly over a column or a pilaster, and all its details, and those of the vase which it sustains, and the balusters A, and B, should be drawn from the same scale of minutes with the column and pilaster.

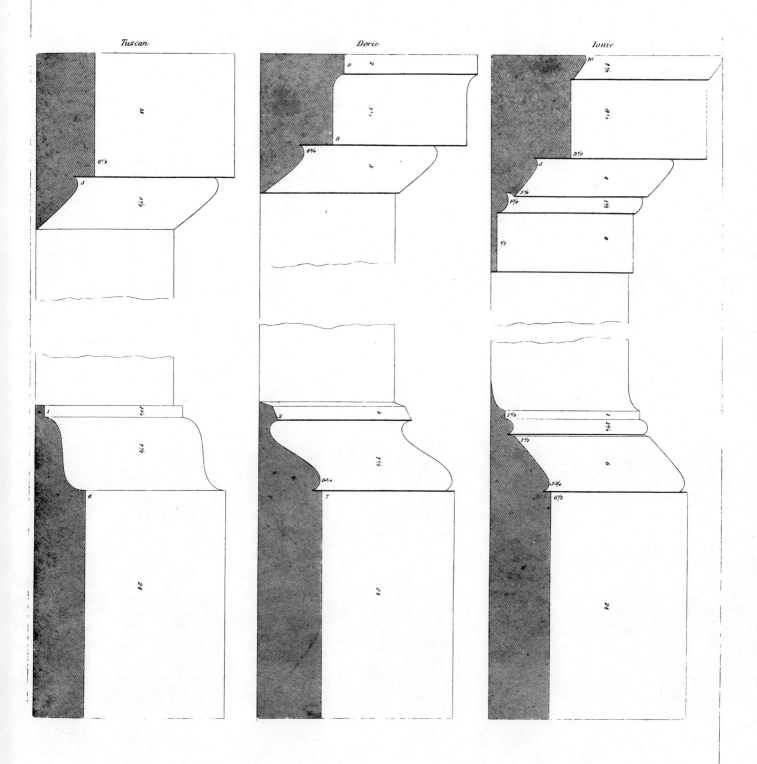

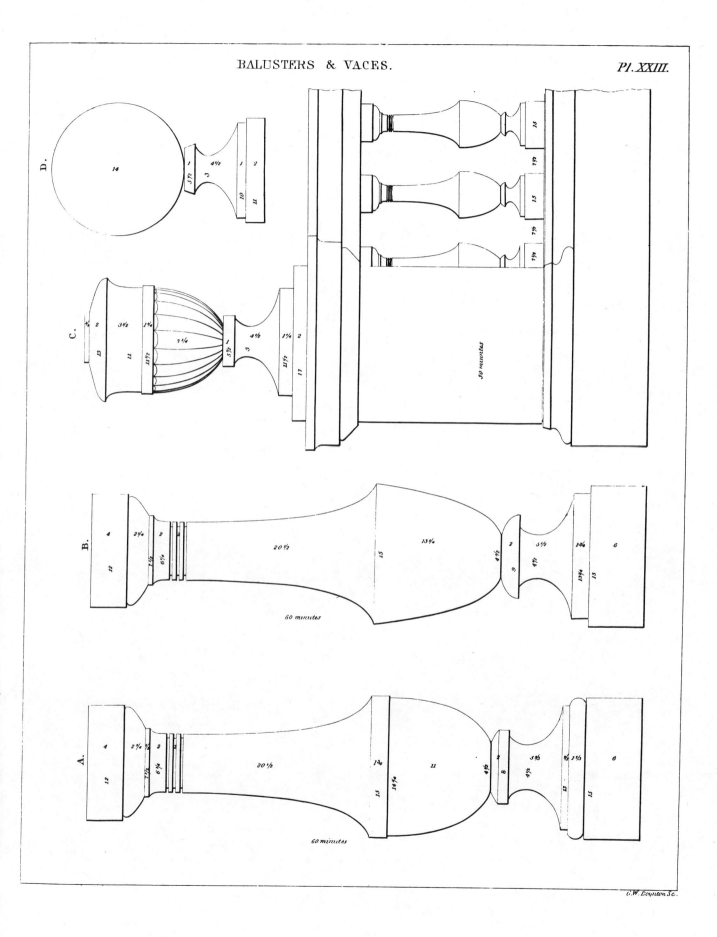

FRONTISPIECES.

PLATE XXIV.

Frontispieces are both useful and ornamental, and make an important part of the facade of a building. They are useful, in sheltering the door and those who are obliged to wait at it for admittance, and ornamental, if skill and judgment are used in their construction. Care must be taken as to the kind and quantity of the decorations employed upon them, that they be neither too profusely nor too sparingly used, and that they be such as to harmonize with the other parts of the front. The door is usually located in the centre of the facade, through which all must pass who enter the building; which circumstance subjects the frontispiece to a severer scrutiny, than the other parts of the same front, and it will therefore be proper and expedient to give to it a greater portion of decorations.

On this Plate is exhibited an example of a frontispiece, without side-lights, depending upon the glass over the door, for the admission of light into the entry. In such cases, the frontispiece is apt to appear insufficient in breadth, particularly, when the front of the building, where it is located, is of very considerable extent. The ample breadth given to the jambs, on each side of the door, in this example, is for the purpose of relieving that defect.

The details of the elevation are figured thereon in feet and inches, beside which, a scale of feet and inches is delineated below it, by which all the various parts may be measured. A, exhibits a plan of the door, its jambs and architraves; B, a section of the door, the threshhold, the impost, which separates the door from the window, and the architraves, also an elevation of the architrave, jamb of the door, and console. C, exhibits the same plan as A, on an enlarged scale; D, the manner of terminating the frett at its upper extremity.

Plate XXV.

A, exhibits an elevation of a frontispiece, every part of which may be measured by the scale of feet and inches annexed; B, an accurate plan of all parts of the frontispiece; C, a section of the entablature, inside architrave, capital to antae, impost, sash, door and threshold, also a side view of the antae or pilaster, to which the door hangs, and the console. Place the fascia of the capital to the antae, which extends from antae to antae, in a vertical line over the greatest projection of the consoles. D, represents a section of the threshold and lower extremity of the door, on a large scale, and also the manner of connecting them, so as to prevent the falling water from passing between them into the house.

Plate XXVI.

On this Plate are represented the plan, elevations and section of an example of a frontispiece, which may be measured by the scale of feet and inches on the preceding Plate. The antae and entablature may be drawn from the scale given on Plate XVIII., and the capital, from that of No. 1, on Plate XVII. The honeysuckles, at the upper extremity of the cornice, are in imitation of those similarly situated on the cornice of the second example of the Corinthian order, Plate XIV.

Plate XXVII.

This Plate exhibits the plans and elevations of a frontispiece of a richer character than either of those preceding, the door being recessed a sufficient distance into the house, to permit columns to be placed between the antaes. This example can be adopted, only when the building is of such extent, as to require the different portions of the facade to be large and strongly marked

FRONTISPEICE.

Pl.XXIV.

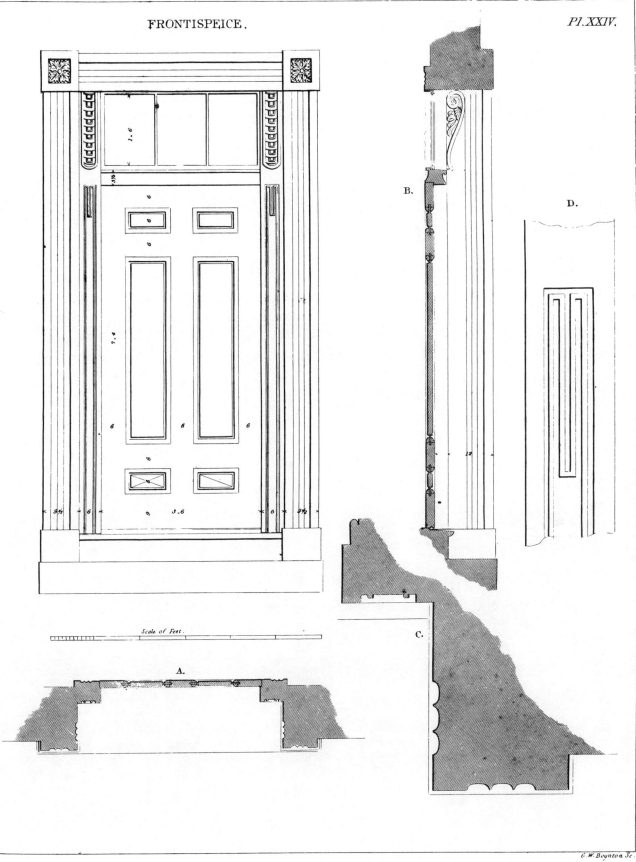

Scale of Feet.

A.

B.

C.

D.

G.W.Boynton Sc.

Pl. XXV.

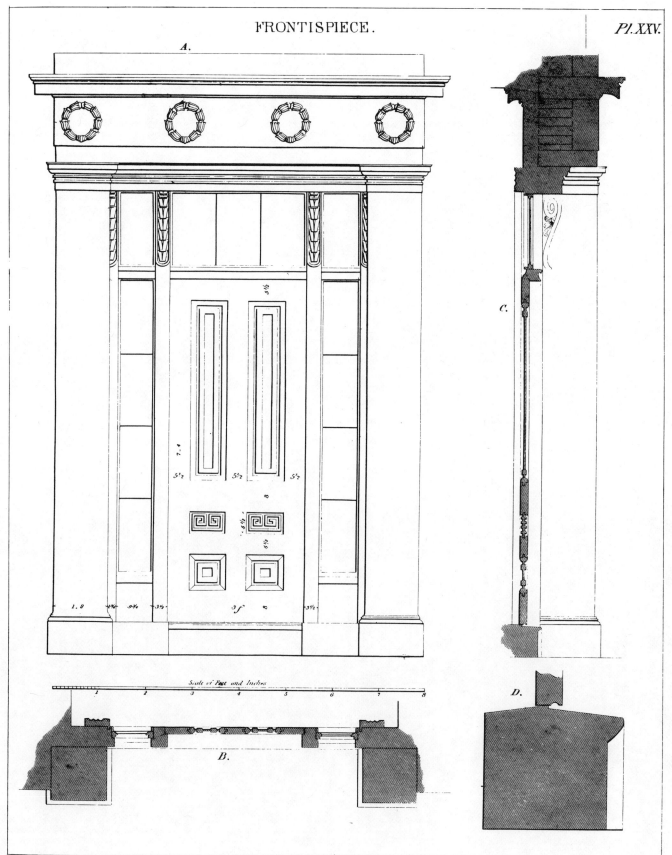

A.

Scale of Feet and Inches

B.

C.

D.

FRONTISPIECE.

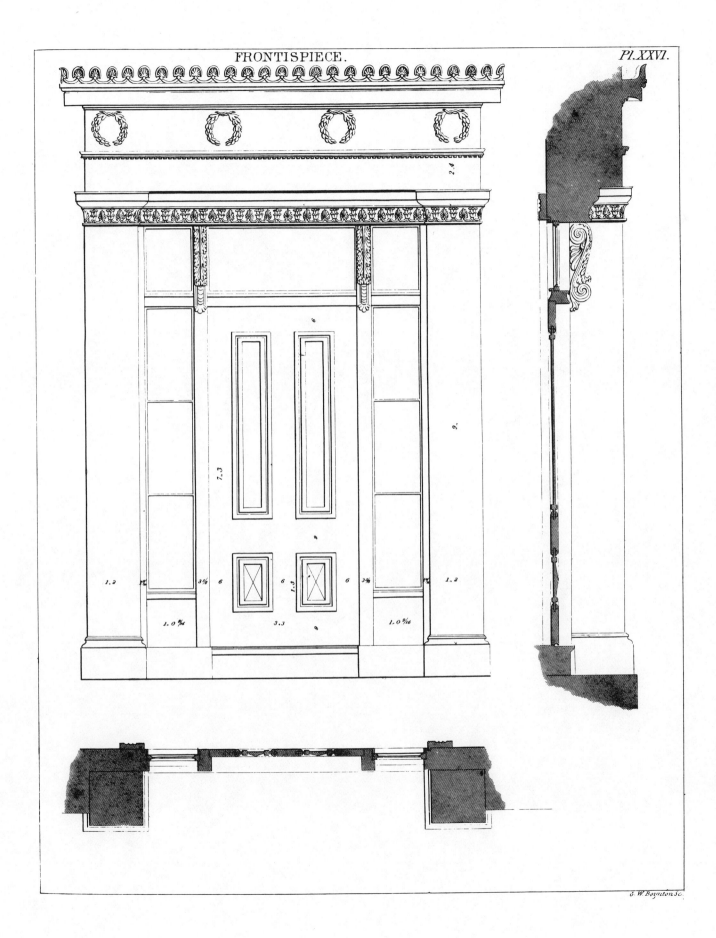

Pl. XXVII.

Scale of Ft. & In.

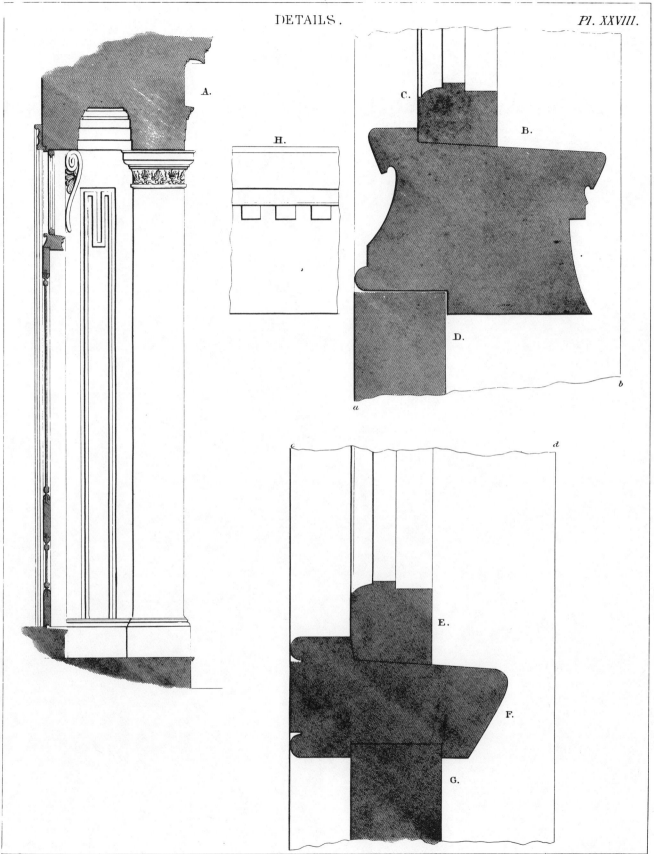

A.

H.

C.

B.

D.

a

b

c

d

E.

F.

G.

G. W. Boynton Sc.

in character. The columns, entablature and antaes are taken from the second example of the Ionic order, Plate IX.

Plate XXVIII.

This Plate exhibits sections of the entablature, door, architrave, impost, threshold, &c.; also an elevation of the antae, the panel between the antaes, part of the pilaster between the door and side-lights, and the console and architrave over it. B, shows a working plan of the impost drawn at one-half of the full size; C, the bottom rail of the sash and its connection with the impost; D, a portion of the door shut into the rabbet; H, a front elevation of the impost; E, a section of the sash rail; F, the sill to the sash frame; and G, the panel. *a b*, shows the depth of the pilaster adjoining the door; *c d*, that adjoining the sash.

Plates XXIX. and XXX.

On these Plates are exhibited the plans, elevations, and sections of a portico of the Corinthian order, taken from the third example of that order.

It will be seen that the floor of this portico has ample breadth, which is obtained, not by a great projection of the columns from the building, but by recessing the door and side-lights into it. We thus avoid that very common fault, of projecting small porticoes to an improper distance from the building, which gives the portico an unstable appearance, as if a small jostle would cause it to totter and fall, arising from its having no other apparent support from the building, than what it obtains by butting against it. But when the door and its appendages are recessed twelve or more inches back from the line of the building, so that a strongly marked shadow is produced, and the entablature and ceiling of the portico are firmly united with the building, the whole appears firm and compact. The fault above-mentioned is not

8

altogether confined to porticos of small dimensions, but may be found in some which are extended the whole breadth and height of the building; for instance, in those where the antaes at the angles of the building project only about three or four inches, as is commonly the case, and the floor of the portico is simply butted against the building, in which case they fail to present that appearance of one perfect whole which is demanded. This defect may be avoided by giving to the antaes a projection on the side facing the columns, equal, at least, to the diameter of the column.

Plate XXXI.

One or more doors are essential to every separate apartment. No door can conveniently be made of a less size than two feet in breadth and six feet in height, that being the smallest space through which a man of ordinary dimensions can freely pass; nor ought the size of a single door to exceed four feet six inches in breadth, and eight feet six inches or nine feet in height. When large external doors are required for public buildings, they are generally divided vertically in the centre, and made to open in two parts, and if they are so high as to cause too great an opening in that direction, they are also divided horizontally, and the upper part being made stationary, the lower opens in two parts as before. No fixed rule is applicable to the proportion of doors. They should be proportioned according to the uses for which they are intended. In a room seventeen feet wide, by twenty-three or four feet long, and twelve and one-half feet in height, the doors should be about three feet three inches wide, and about seven feet nine inches high. When sliding doors are used, they should have something more than twice the breadth of the other doors in the same room, and be two feet higher, depending, in that respect, upon the height of the room, and upon the ornaments used to decorate them.

No. 1.

No. 2.

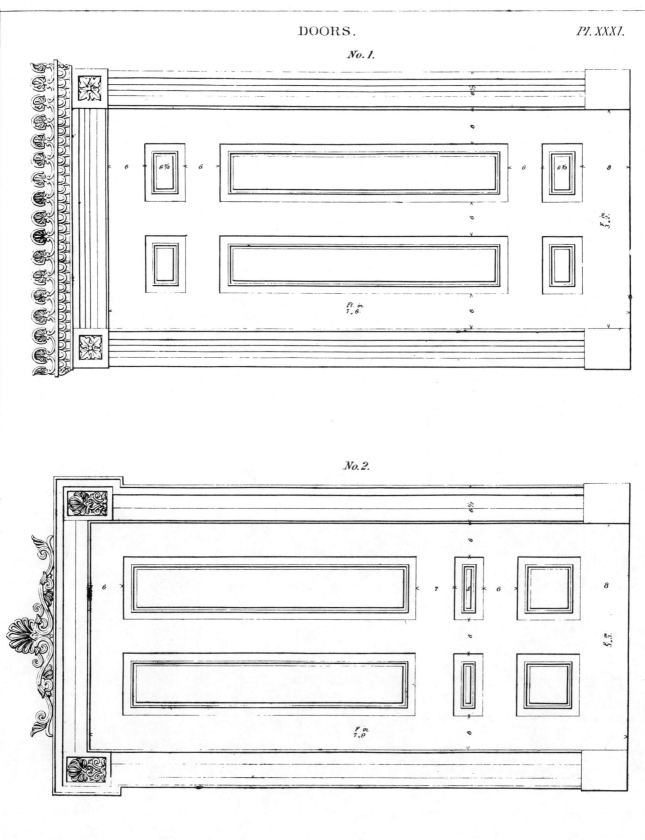

SLIDING DOORS.

Pl. XXXII.

Scale of Feet and Inches

G.W. Boynton Sc.

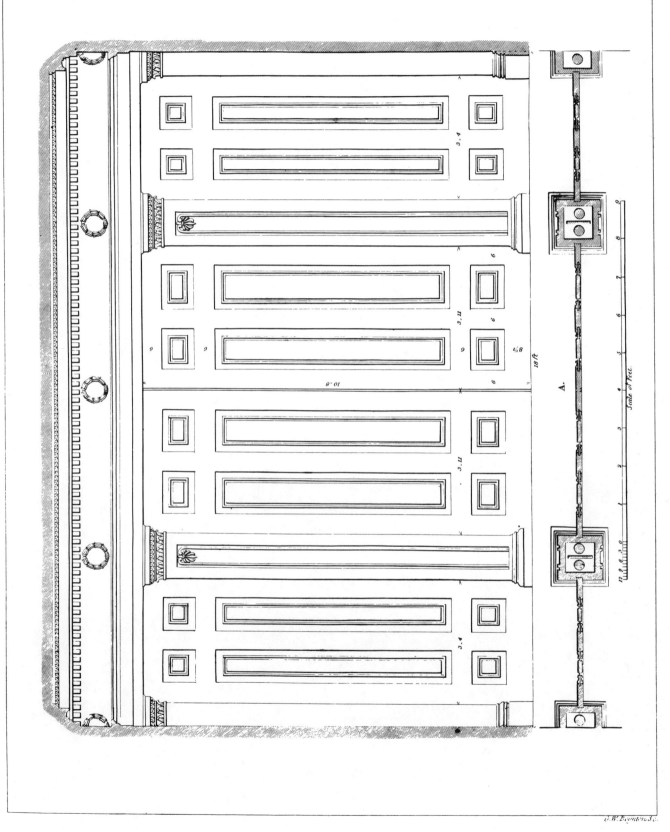

On this Plate are exhibited two designs for doors, intended for inside finishing. The details of each are figured thereon in feet and inches. The architrave of No. 1, is taken from No. 9, on Plate XLI.; and that of No. 2, from No. 6, on the same Plate. The sculpture on each of these architraves may and ought to be left off, when the finish of the room is of such a character as not to require it.

Plate XXXII.

On this Plate are exhibited a pair of sliding doors, with a scale of feet and inches annexed. The architrave and its decorations are drawn to match those of No. 2, on Plate XXXI., but on an extended scale, both of them being intended for the same room.

Plate XXXIII.

On this Plate is an example designed for a suit of doors extending across the room. They are designed to slide up into the room above them, until entirely concealed by the entablature, leaving nothing to divide the two rooms except the antaes.

This kind of communication between two rooms, will often be found very convenient, particularly in hotels, where it may sometimes be desirable to use the two rooms as a dining room. In such a case, the table will be set in the centre, and the waiters will pass between the two side antaes.

A, shows a section of antaes, doors, and weights by which the doors are hung, also a scale of feet and inches, by which any part of this design may be measured.

The entablature is taken from the example of an antae and entablature on Plate XX.

Plate XXXIV.

On this Plate are exhibited three different examples of mouldings and paneling for doors, and three also for shutters, all of which are drawn at full size for practice, representing a section of each moulding and a part of the style and panel of each example, and also the method of connecting the style, panel and moulding.

WINDOWS.

Plate XXXV.

This Plate exhibits various sections of the sash frames, shutters, &c. for the finish of two windows. No. 1, shows a section of the finish of a window, the shutters of which are designed to fold against the wall ;— a, represents the architrave; b, the grounds; c, the jamb casing; d, face casing to the sash frame and back lining; $e\ e$, the shutters; f, the hanging style; g, the pulley style to the sash frame; h, the face casing; k, the parting bead; j, the moulding to the sash frame; m, the bead; l, the style of the sash; $i\ i$, weights. No. 2, is nearly the same with No. 1, the principal difference consisting in the shutters, in the former folding into the wall, and therefore requiring to be made thicker than in the latter case. No. 3, shows a section of the bottom rail to a sash and a sash bar. No. 4, shows a top rail and sash bar, with a moulding differing from that of No. 3. No. 5, shows the meeting rails of the sash, and the method of connecting them together. The last three examples are drawn one-half their full size, and Nos. 1 and 2, on a scale of one-fourth of an inch, to one inch.

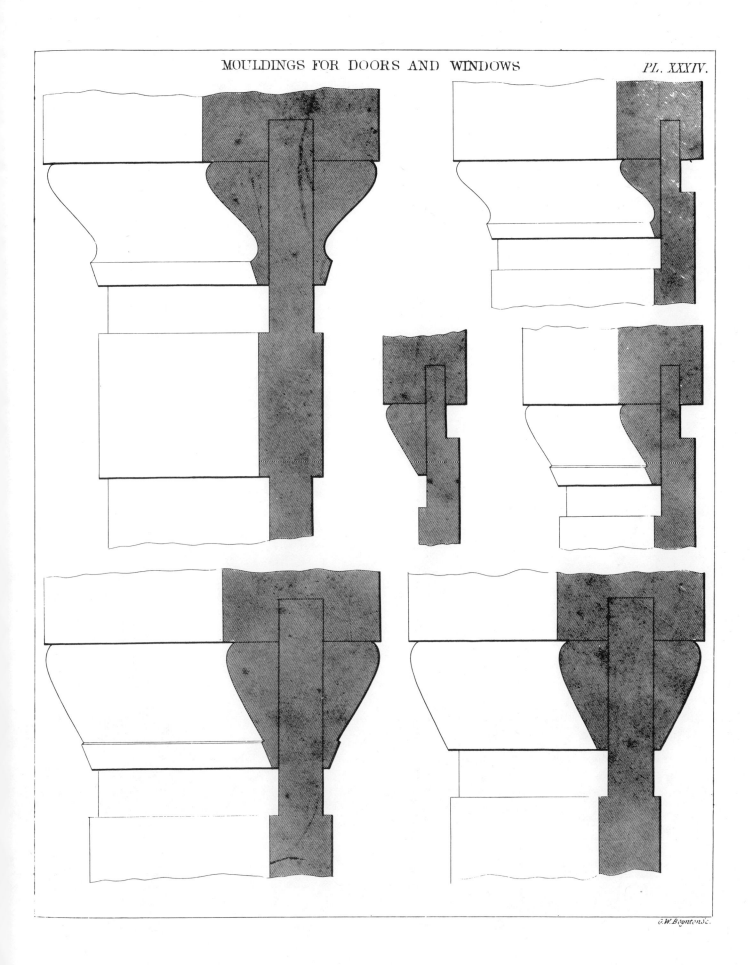

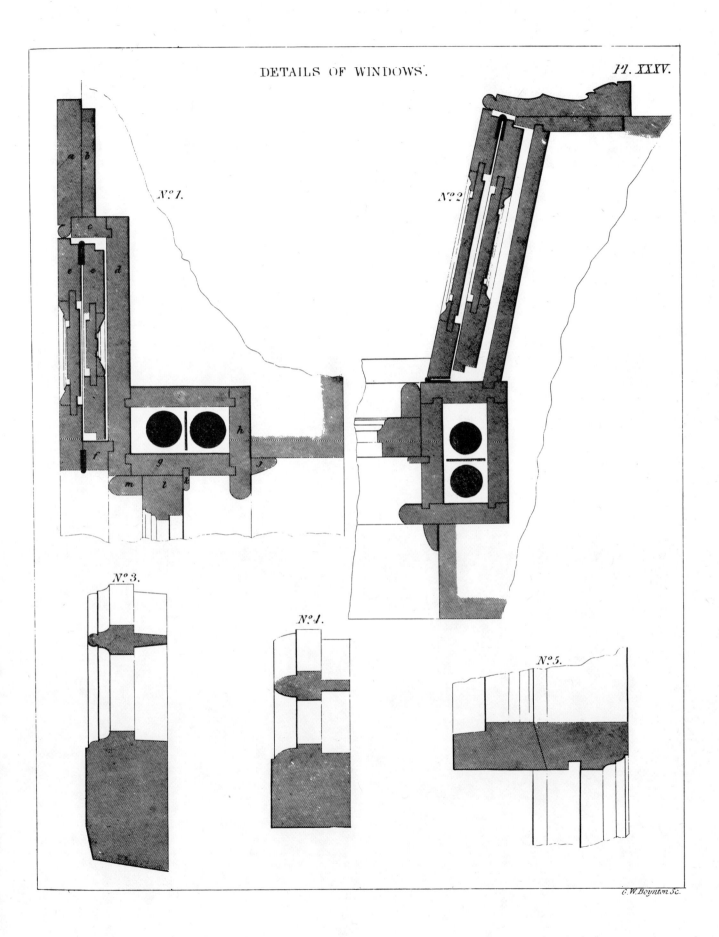

C.W.Boynton Sc.

Pl. XXXVI.

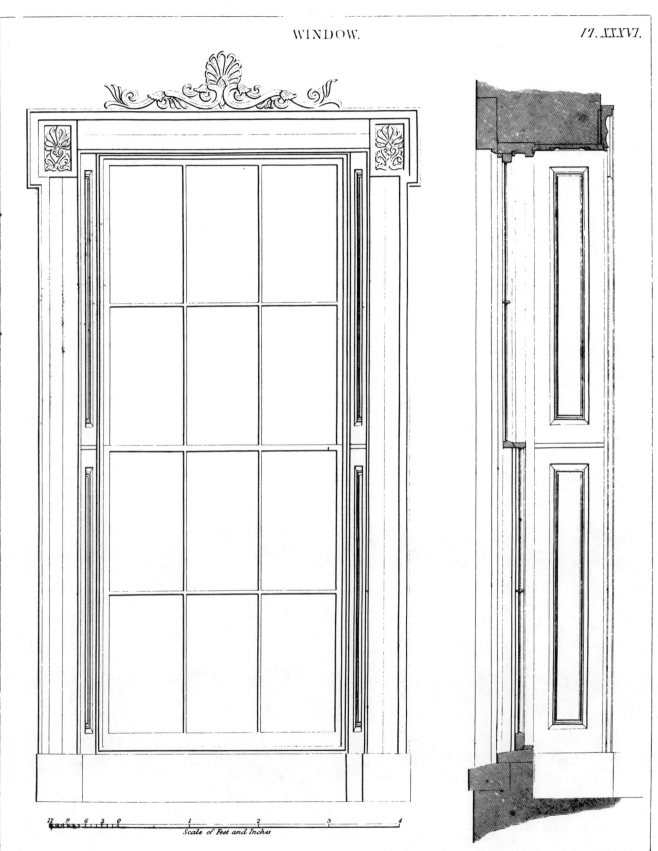

Scale of Feet and Inches

E.W. Boynton Sc.

WINDOWS.

Pl. XXXVII.

No. 1.

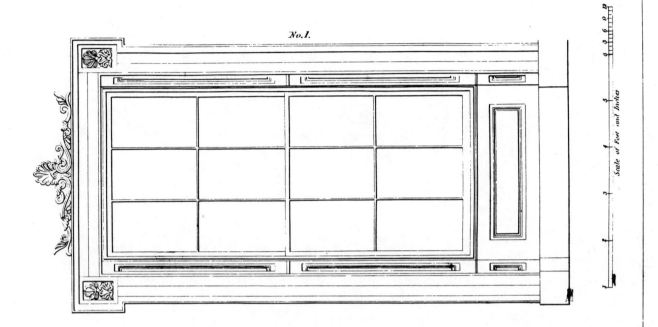

Scale of Feet and Inches

No. 2.

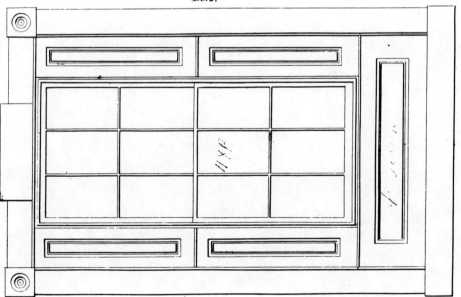

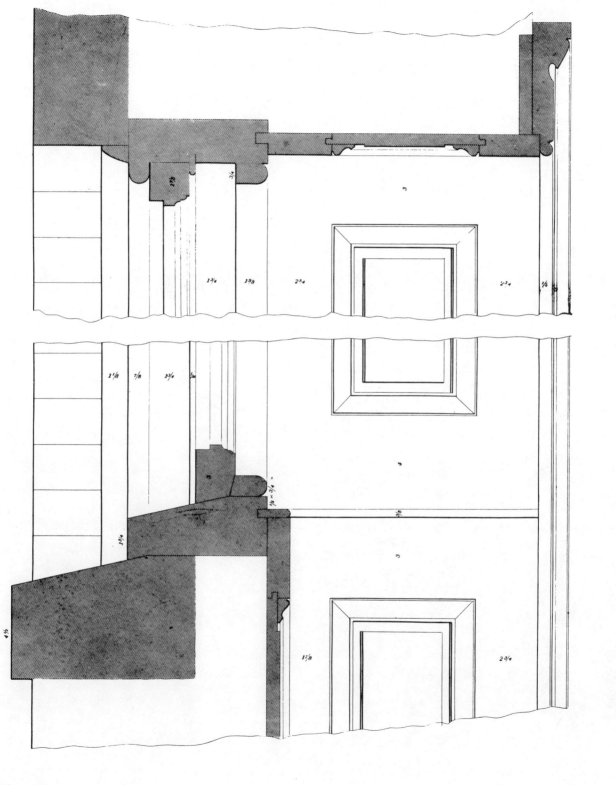

Plate XXXVI.

This Plate exhibits a front and side elevation of a window extending down to the floor. Its architrave and decorations are similar to those of door No. 2, on Plate XXXI., and are intended for the same room.

Plate XXXVII.

On this Plate are the elevations of two windows, showing the internal finish of each. The plan of No. 1, will be found at No. 2, on Plate XXXV. It will be seen that this window is finished with a panel under it, in the common way, and the architrave and sculpture attached to it are intended to match those of the door No. 2, on Plate XXXI. No. 2, shows an elevation of plan No. 1, on Plate XXXV., the shutters of which fold upon the wall. The architrave, and a tablet over the window, are without mouldings.

Plate XXXVIII.

On this Plate are exhibited the sections of the window sills, bottom rail to the sash, bead to the sash frame, back with its bead, cap of the sash frame, top rail to the sash, soffit, architrave grounds, &c.. It also shows an elevation of the shutters, sash frame, &c., all drawn on a scale of one-fourth of an inch to an inch, and figured in inches.

PEDIMENTS.

The beauty of the pediment depends very much upon the relative proportion of its base, to its vertical height or pitch. The ancient Greek pediments, which· surmounted the temples and porticos, were generally of a very low pitch.   That of the temple of Theseus, was about one-eighth of its base line.   That of the Ionic temple, situated on the banks of the river Ilissus, and that of the Doric portico, were each about one-seventh, and that of the temple of the Winds, about one-fifth.   It appears, from a comparison of these examples, that a ratio existed between the extension of the base, and the height of the pediment.

Suppose the base of a pediment to be twelve feet, and its pitch one-eighth of the same, or eighteen inches.   If we deduct from the pitch the depth of the inclined cornice, very little remains for the vertical height of the tympanum of the pediment ; and therefore a pitch of one-fifth would be preferable in this case.   But suppose the base to be extended to fifty feet, and the pitch to be one-fifth or ten feet.   This height would give to the pediment too much consequence, making that a principal in the composition which should be subordinate, its office being to protect and shelter the building which sustains it ; in the latter case, therefore, one-eighth would be preferable.

Plate XXXIX.

On this Plate are exhibited the plan and elevations of a French window. It is divided vertically in the centre, and opens in two parts, like doors. When it is of a sufficient height to permit the top lights to be made a fixture, it will be advisable to divide it horizontally, making the meeting rails, in that case, like the meeting stiles.

Plate XL.

This Plate exhibits the details of a French window, the subject of the preceding Plate.—*a*, at No. 1, shows a section of the cap to the sash frame ; *b*, part of the soffit ; *d*, window cap ; *c*, top rail to sash ; *e*, bottom rail ; *f*, a piece of cast iron, screwed to the under surface of the rail ; *g*, another piece of cast iron, screwed to the window sill, the upper surface of

FRENCH WINDOW.

Pl. XXXIX.

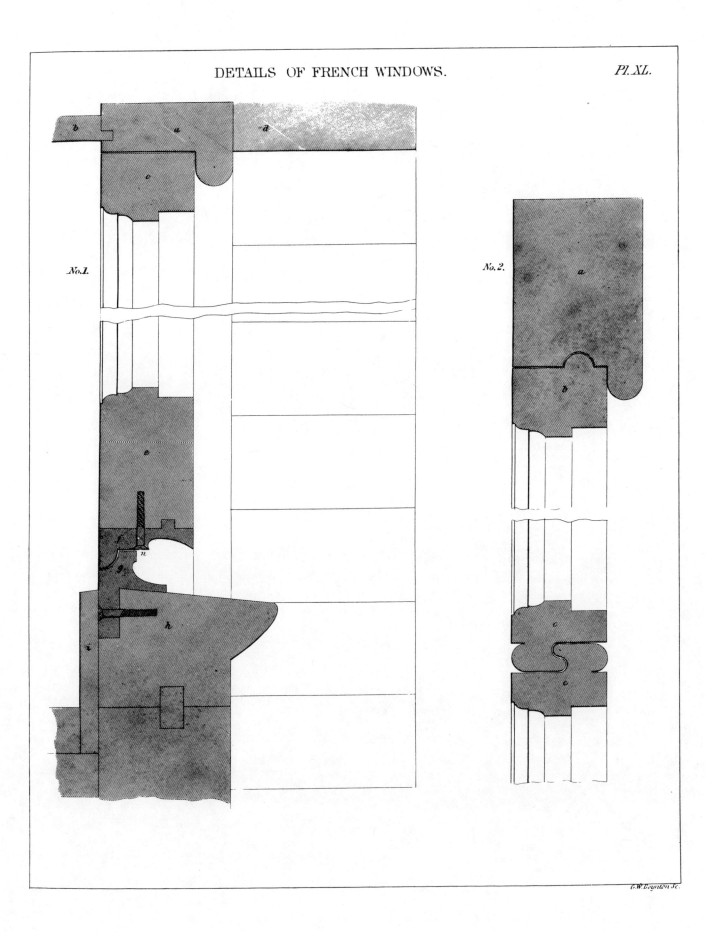

No. 1.

No. 2.

G. W. Boynton Sc.

which coincides with the under surface of *f*. It must be observed that the projection of this moulding, at *n*, must not be equal to that of *o*, at the bottom of the rabate, between the meeting stiles, shown at No. 2; in order that the water driving into and passing down the rabate, which otherwise might be forced by the wind into the house, may fall at a little distance before *n*, to the window sill. *h*, shows the window sill; *i*, the plinth; *a*, on No. 2, shows the section of the jamb to the sash frame; *b*, that of the sash stile; *c* and *c*, meeting stiles to sash. These details are all drawn at one-half their full size.

ARCHITRAVES.

Plate XLI.

No member of the orders is more in use than the architrave. Doors, windows, niches, arcades, &c. are all more or less indebted to it for their dressings. It is therefore highly important that its proportions should be adapted to the place which it occupies, and that it should accord with the finish of the rest of the apartment. The following rule has been adopted by some authors, to determine the breadth of architraves. Make the breadth of the architrave equal to that which would be required in the entablature of a column, of the same height with the aperture, around which the architrave is employed.

Another rule, more generally practised, is to make the breadth of the architrave one-sixth part of that of the aperture. But both of these rules will require to be varied in many situations. For instance, if the door is three feet wide, one-sixth of this, or six inches, would be a good proportion; but by the same rule, a pair of sliding doors, seven feet four inches wide, in the same room, would have an architrave about fourteen and six-tenths inches wide, which would be a proportion altogether inadmissible. In such a case, one-tenth of the breadth of the door would be a proper proportion.

These examples are drawn one-half the full size for common practice. Nos. 1, 2, 3, and 4, are single, and Nos. 5, 6, and 7, double architraves. Nos. 8, 9, and 10, are what is called pilaster architraves.

Plate XLII.

On this Plate are six designs for base mouldings, differing in form, but not much in size. They are drawn one-half the full size for practice, each part being one-eighth of an inch. If they are drawn from a common two foot rule, calling one-fourth of an inch one part, a suitable size for common practice will be produced.

STUCCO CORNICES.

Plate XLIII.

The object of these cornices is ornament, and is obtained only where their size and form are in perfect accordance with the extent and character of the apartment, in which they are placed. In all other cases, the money expended upon them is wasted; and care should therefore be used that they be not defective in that particular.

The following simple rule, which makes the height of the cornice a certain portion of the height of the room, will serve to assist the judgment; but circumstances will often occur, requiring some deviation. If the room in which either of the examples of Nos. 1 or 2, are to be employed, be eleven feet in height, make the height of either example equal to nine-tenths of an inch, for every foot in the height of the room, or nine and nine-tenths inches.

Pl. XLI.

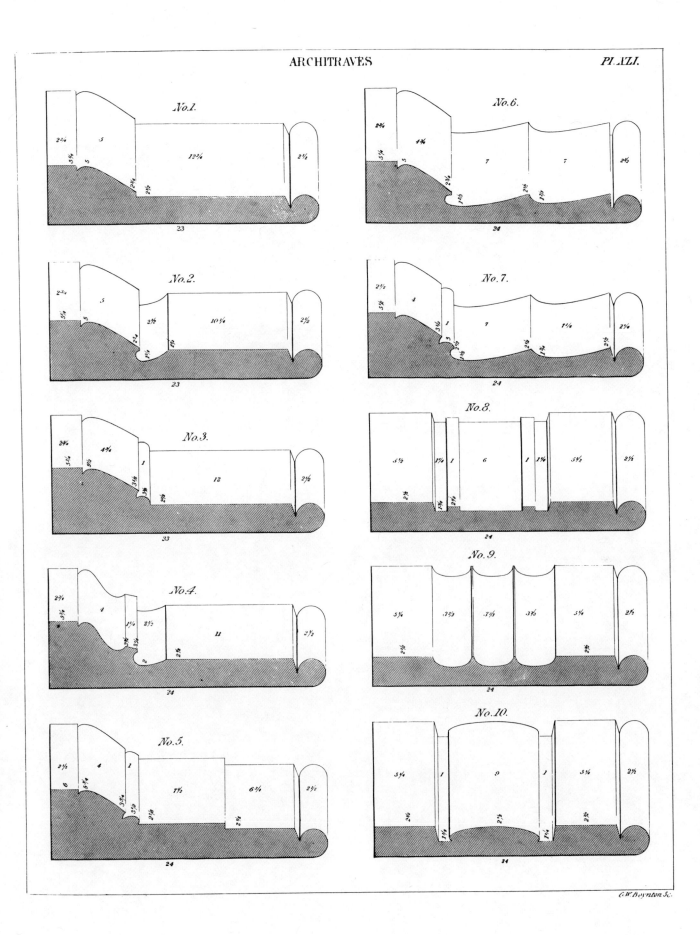

No.1.

No.6.

No.2.

No.7.

No.3.

No.8.

No.4.

No.9.

No.5.

No.10.

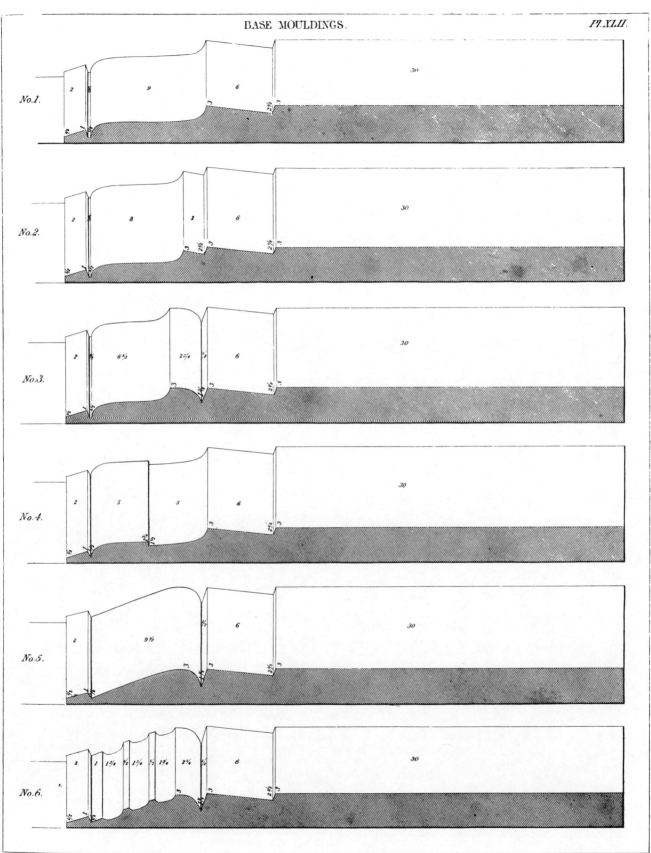

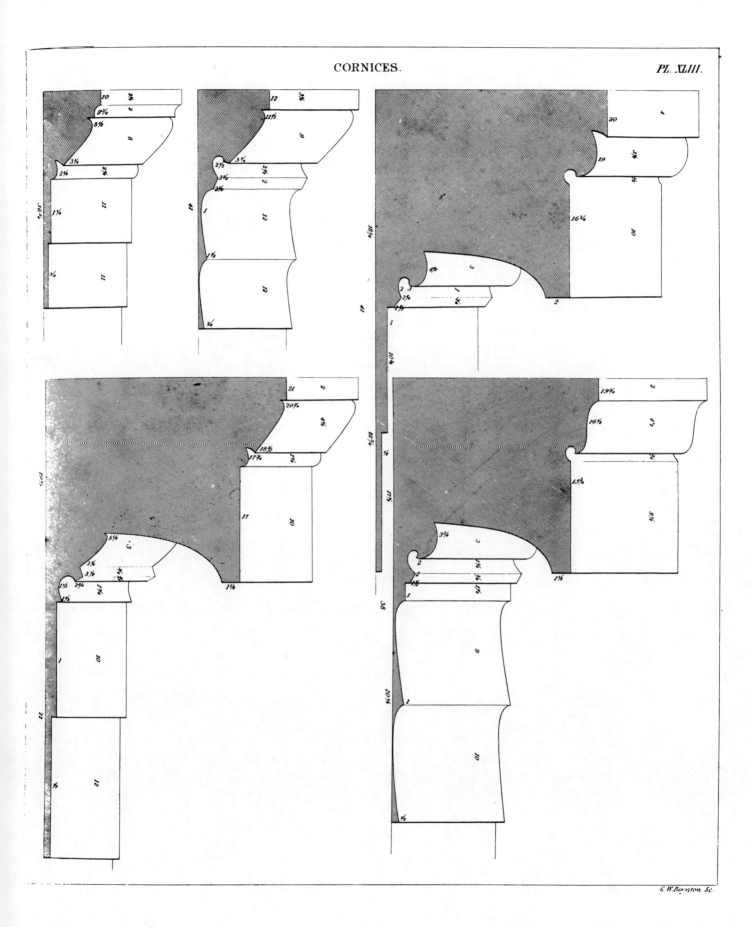

In a room of the same height exclusive of the frieze, the height of either of the examples 3, 4, and 5, might be four-tenths of an inch to each foot in that of the room, or four and four-tenths inches.

EAVE CORNICES.

PLATE XLIV.

Eave Cornices are not only ornamental, but useful; for while they serve to crown and protect the building, the gutters placed in them receive the water which falls upon the roof, and carry it to a point whence it may descend to the ground.

A frieze may be added to the under surface, where a sufficient space is left between the cornice and the top of the window to admit it without the appearance of being crowded; and in this case, the windows lighting the attic may be so concealed by the frieze, as to appear ornamental, by decorating their front with the frett, or enclosing them with the wreath.

The most difficult thing, in relation to these cornices, is to determine a correct proportion for them in the various situations in which they may be required. The nature of the surface, on which the building stands, the extent of the front, the character of the building, and many other circumstances, often require in practice a deviation from any regular rule. It is obvious that a cornice of a suitable size for a tower twenty-five feet square, and sixty feet high, will not be large enough for a building of the same height, but with the sides extended to one hundred feet. I have given below a kind of table, by which the depth of the cornices on buildings from eighty to a hundred feet may be obtained, subject to such corrections as a regard to the observations above made upon the subject may require.

10

Suppose it be required to obtain the depth of a cornice, situated at a height of fifteen feet. Make the cornice twenty-fortieths of an inch for each foot in that height, or seven and thirty-five fortieths inches.

The following table may be used in other cases.

Height of building, 20 ft. $\frac{19}{40}$ inches per foot, or $9\frac{20}{40}$ inches.

"   "   25 ft. $\frac{18}{40}$ "   " $11\frac{10}{40}$ inches.

"   "   30 ft. $\frac{17}{40}$ "   " $12\frac{30}{40}$ inches.

"   "   40 ft. $\frac{16}{40}$ "   "   16   inches.

"   "   50 ft. $\frac{15}{40}$ "   " $18\frac{30}{40}$ inches.

"   "   60 ft. $\frac{14}{40}$ "   "   21   inches.

"   "   70 ft. $\frac{13}{40}$ "   " $22\frac{30}{40}$ inches.

"   "   80 ft. $\frac{12}{40}$ "   "   24   inches.

CONSOLES.

PLATES XLV. AND XLVI.

This ancient and highly ornamented member of architecture seems to have been neglected in all the late practical works on this subject, with the exception of one example, very beautiful and richly decorated, taken from the great door of the Grecian temple, Erechtheus, at Athens. This however is not adapted to our every day practice, in its form, decorations, or expense of execution. I have therefore presented several examples of the console which accord with the fashion of the day, differing from each other in form and decorations, beginning with those the most simple, and ending with others highly ornamented. I have taken care to arrange the sculpture, in such a manner that three of these examples may be cut by a common carpenter, without the aid of a carver. D, on Plate XLV., exhibits a side view, and C, a cross section of Fig. 1, taken from A to B; E, represents a side view;

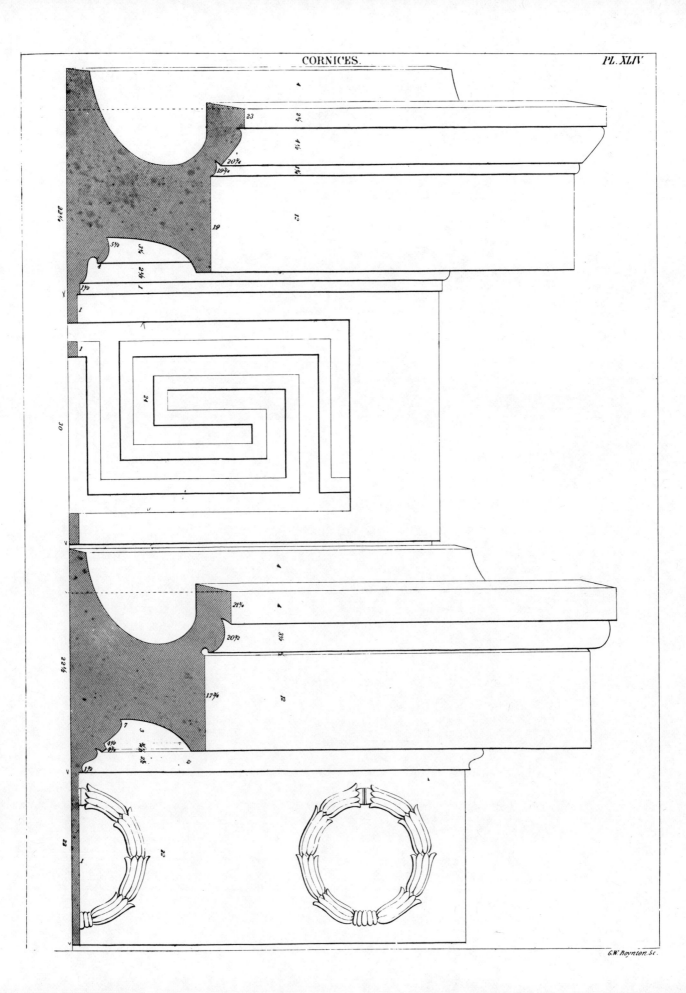

G.W. Boynton Sc.

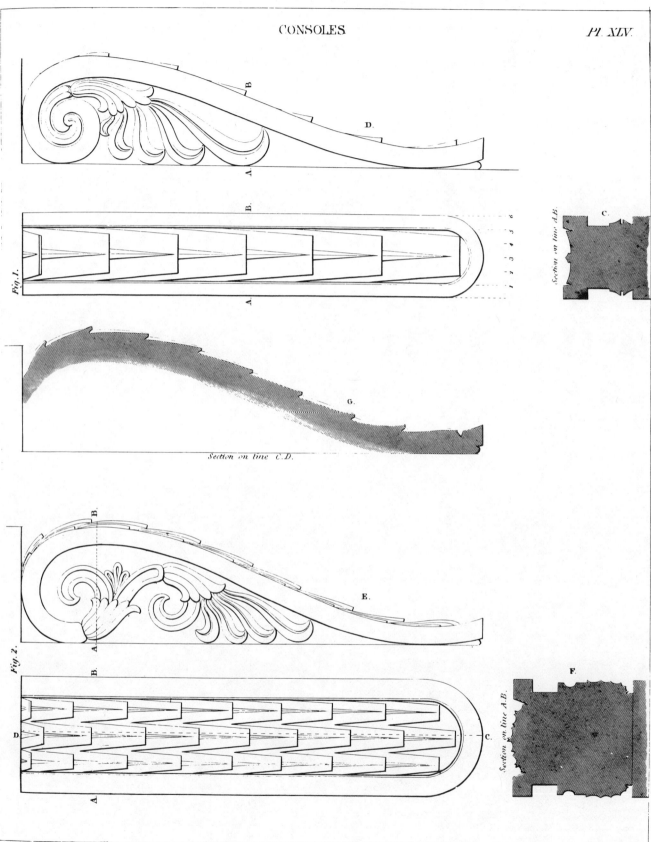

Fig. 1.

Section on line A.B. C.

Section on line C.D.

Fig. 2.

Section on line A.B. F.

G.W. Boynton Sc.

Pl. XLVI.

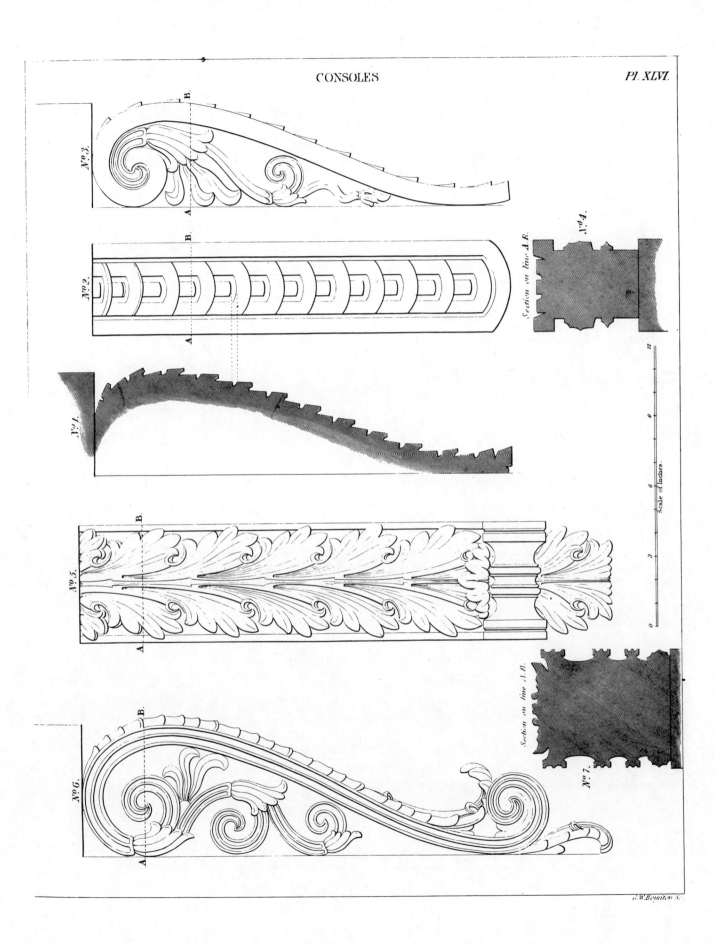

Nº 3.

B.

A.

Section on line A.B.

Nº 4.

Nº 2.

B.

A.

Nº 1.

12

0

Scale of Inches.

6

3

0

Nº 5.

B.

A.

Section on line A.B.

Nº 7.

Nº 6.

B.

A.

C.W.Boynton S.

CENTREPEICE.

PL.XLVII.

N°1.

N°2.

G.W.Boynton Sc.

No 1.

No 2.

Scale of Feet

E.W.Boynton Sc.

and F, a cross section taken from A to B, on Fig. 2. No. 3, on Plate XLVI., exhibits a side view; and No. 4, a cross section of No. 2. No. 6, shows a side view of No. 5; and No. 7, a cross section taken from A to B. No. 1, is a vertical section of No. 5.

Plate XLVII.

This Plate contains an example of a centre piece, figured in inches. No. 2, represents a section of the mouldings and frett, which encircle the flower in the centre. They are drawn at one-half their full size, and figured in parts.— *a*, is in a line with the ceiling of the room; and *c*, in a line with the centre piece.

The lower part of this Plate contains three examples of fretts, one for a guiloche, and one for a leaf ornament, all of which will be handsome when suited to the place which they occupy. The shaded parts, *a*, *b*, *c*, *d*, *e*, are sections of the figures against which they are respectively drawn.

Plate XLVIII.

This Plate exhibits a design for a shop front, suitable for either town or country. The pilaster and entablature may be made of stone or wood, according to the taste or convenience of the proprietor.

The small windows between the capitals of the pilasters are intended to be secured with a frett, made of iron, instead of shutters, so that, if the shop should take fire in the night time, the accident may be more easily discovered, by the light shining through these windows; and in the same manner, a robber might perhaps be detected, if he should enter the shop in the night for plunder, and use a lantern for his purposes. The doors may be recessed so far back, as to show the whole thickness of the pilaster; but it will be wise, in order to show the goods within to the best advantage, to place the window in such a position, that the front surface of the shutter, when closed, may be in the same place with the front of the pilasters.

STAIRS.

Every building, consisting of more than one story, is indebted to this portion of architecture for ornament, as well as utility. The height, breadth, and length of the steps, should be proportioned to the situation and use for which they are constructed. This remark, however, is subject to this qualification, that the height should never exceed eight inches, nor the breadth fifteen inches. Every workman is supposed to have a sufficient knowledge of all kinds of stairs, except those on a circular plan. The method most practiced, of forming the circular part of the rail without a cylinder, is comparatively of recent date. To the ingenious Peter Nicholson, of London, we are all indebted for this method. It was invented by him and published in the year 1792, and since that time it has wonderfully extended itself into practice. In the year 1795, I made the drawings and superintended the erection of a circular staircase in the State House at Hartford, Connecticut, which, I believe, was the first circular rail that was ever made in New England. This rail was glued up around a cylinder, in pieces of about one-eighth of an inch thick. Since the first discovery of the true principles of hand railing, Mr. Nicholson has made several important improvements, for one of which, about seventeen or eighteen years since, the Society of Arts in London awarded him a gold medal. This improvement renders the subject the most simple and direct of any of his methods. I have therefore adopted it as my model here, with some trifling deviations.

Plate XLIX.

This Plate exhibits two examples for scrolls, which terminate the lower extremity of hand rails; one of a curtail step, and one of a newell.

In order to describe the scroll, Fig. 1, make a circle of three and one-half

Pl. 49.

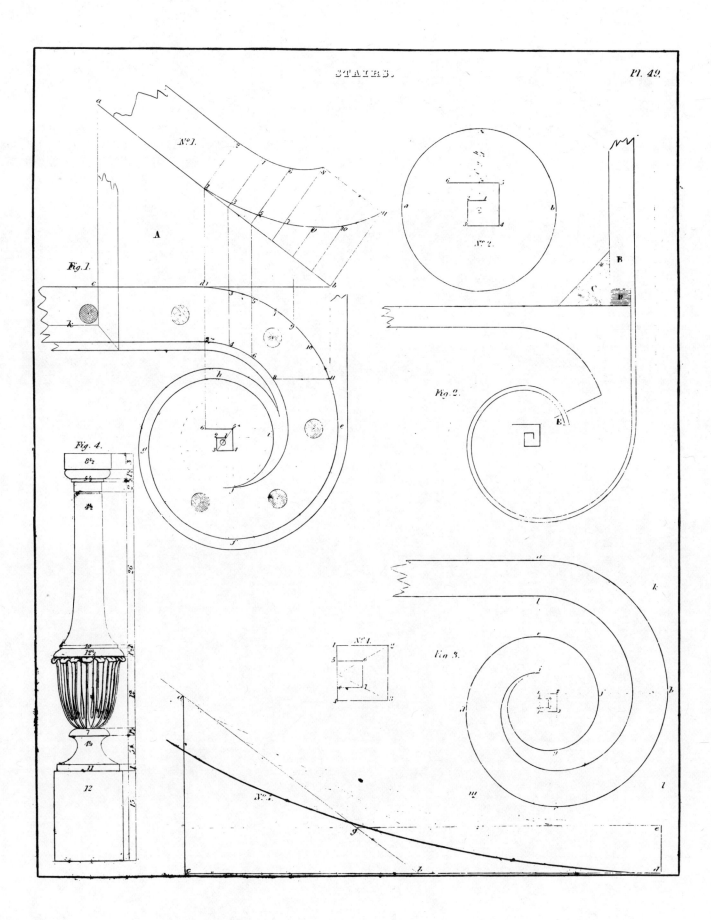

Fig. 1.

Fig. 2.

Fig. 3.

Fig. 4.

inches in diameter, as is shown by dotted lines. To illustrate this subject in a clear and distinct manner, the circle is repeated on a larger scale at No. 2. Divide the circle in the centre by the horizontal line *a o b;* draw the vertical line *o e;* divide *o e* into three equal parts at *c, d, e;* through the point *c* draw 6 *c* 5, parallel to *a b.* Divide *c d* into three equal parts at *f, g, h,* and make *c* 6 equal to *o f.* Then from the point 6, and through the centre *o,* draw the diagonal line 6 *o* 4, and intersect it at right angles by another diagonal line passing through the centre *o,* and cutting 6 5 at 5. At right angles with 6 5, draw 5 4, cutting 6 *o* 4 at 4; and parallel with 6 5, draw 4 3, cutting 5 *o* 3 at 3. Draw 3 2 parallel to 5 4, cutting 6 *o* 4 at 2; and 2 1 parallel to 6 5, cutting 5 *o* 3 at 1; which completes the six centres on which the scroll is drawn.' We will now return to Fig. 1. On the centre 1, with the radius 1 *j,* draw *j i;* on the centre 2, with the radius 2 *i,* draw *i h;* on 3, with the radius 3 *h,* draw *h g;* on 4, with the radius 4 *g,* draw *g f;* on 5, with the radius 5 *f,* draw *f e;* on 6, draw *e d;* which completes the outside circle. The inside line, and also those of the nosing of the steps, are drawn from the same centres.

To draw the face mould, No. 1, the rail is supposed to be glued to the scroll at the line 8 11. A, exhibits the pitch board; *c b,* the base line; and *a b,* the raking line. Divide from *d,* the beginning of the twist, to *b,* into any number of parts, making one intersect the edge of the rail at 8, and another at 11. Then draw these lines across the pitch board to the raking line *a b.* At right angles with *a b,* continue them across the face mould, No. 1. From the line *a b,* make each of the lines 3, 5, 7, 9, 10, and 11, equal to the corresponding lines from the line *d b,* to the edge of the rail 3, 5, 7, 9, 10, and 11. Make also 1 2, 3 4, 5 6, and 7 8, in No. 1, respectively equal to *d* 2, 3 4, 5 6, and 7 8, on Fig. 1. Then through the points 1, 3, 5, 7, 9, 10, and 11, and also through the points 2, 4, 6, and 8, trace the curves; and the face mould is completed.

Fig. 2, exhibits a curtail step drawn from the same centres as that of the rail. B, shows the edge of the riser; C, a block glued to both step and

11

riser; D and E, keys by which the riser is made fast and drawn home to the step. The dotted lines represent the nosing of the step.

To draw the falling mould, No. 5, let *a*, *b* and *c*, be the angles of the pitch board. Produce the base line *c b*, to *d;* make *c d* equal to the stretchout of the scroll on Fig. 1; from *d*, around to *f*, set up the depth of the rail, which is supposed to be two inches, to the line *f g e*. Then divide *a g* and *g e*, each into a like number of equal parts, and form the curve by the intersection of lines. The curve of the lower edge may be obtained by gaging.

Fig. 3, exhibits another method of describing a scroll of two revolutions, the beginning and termination of which are given.—*a*, represents the commencement, and *i*, the termination. Divide *i a* into two equal parts at *l;* subdivide *i l* into one more part than the number of revolutions required, in this case into three parts. Make the square in the centre equal to one of those parts, and construct it like that at No. 4, which is drawn on a large scale. Then on 1, in the square, and with the radius *i a*, draw the quadrant *a b*. On 2, and with the radius 2 *b*, describe *b c;* on 3, with the radius 3 *c*, describe *c d;* on 4, describe *d e;* on 5, describe *e f;* on 6, describe *f g;* on 7, describe *g h;* and on 8, describe *h i;* which completes the outside line. That of the inside is drawn by the same centres.

It is evident by the dotted lines representing the straight part of the rail at *k l* and *m*, that four scrolls of unequal sizes may be obtained by this example.

Fig. 4, exhibits an example of a newell, drawn on a large scale and figured in parts. Its size is supposed to be six inches at the base. Each part would therefore be equal to one-half of an inch. Where there is not a sufficient space in the entry that can be conveniently spared, this newell will be found a good substitute for the scroll.

PLATE L.

To find all the moulds which are necessary for the completion of a stair rail standing over a circular plan, as exhibited at Fig. 1, we proceed as follows:

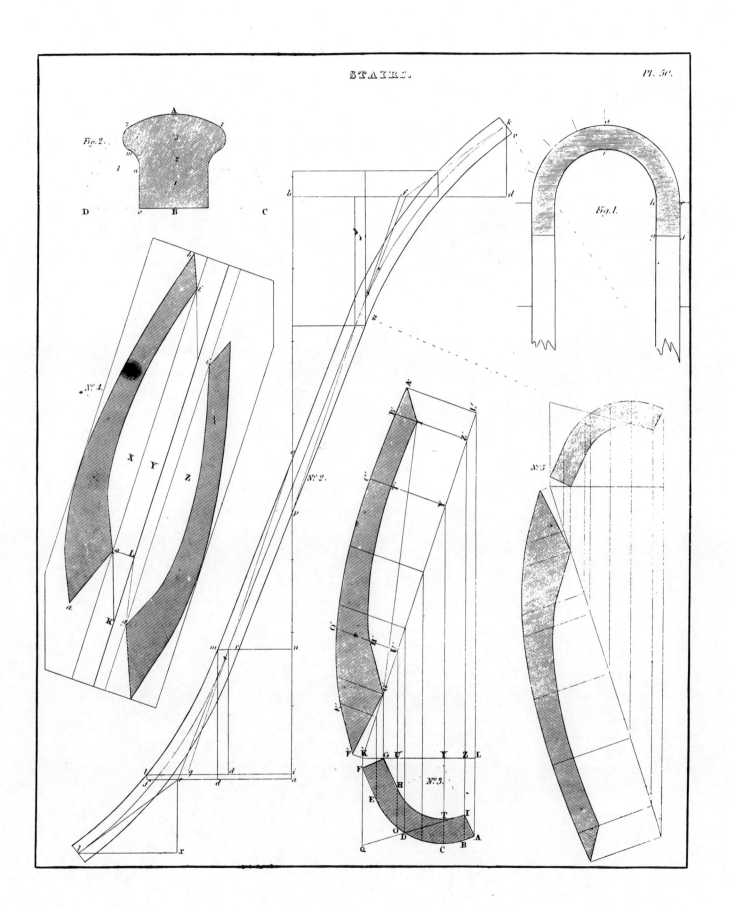

Fig.2.

Fig.1.

Nº 1.

Nº 2.

Nº 3.

Nº 5.

Make *a b*, No. 2, equal to the height of the winders. Draw *a e* and *b f*, at right angles with *a b*; make *e a* and *b f*, each equal to the development of *e a*, Fig. 1; draw *e x* and *d k*, each equal to the height of one step, and parallel to *a b*; make *x l* and *f d*, each equal to the breadth of one step, and join *e l*, *e f*, and *f k*. Make *e t* equal to *e l*, and *f s* equal to *f k*. Then form the curves, or easoffs, by the intersecting of lines, or by producing lines at right angles from the rail, as represented by the dotted lines *u* and *v*, until they meet, and their junction will be the centre for describing the curve. The breadth of the falling mould is generally about two inches; a line, therefore, about one inch above the one here described, and another at the same distance below, will complete the falling mould.

Construction of the Face Mould, No. 3.

Let A D E F G H I, be the plan of the rail, and E F, G H, a portion of the straight part; I, being the upper, F, the lower, and D, the middle resting points. Make the stretchout of A D, equal to that of D F. In the figure of the falling mould, produce the base *a e*, to *f*, *a e* then being equal to the development of A E; make *a d* equal to the development of A D, and *e f* equal to E F. Draw *f l* parallel to *a b*, and cutting the upper side of the falling mould at *l*; parallel to *f a*, draw *l i*, cutting *a b* at *i*; in *i l*, make *i d* equal to I D; draw *d m* parallel to *a b*, cutting the upper side of the falling mould at *m*; draw *m n* parallel to *f a*, cutting *a b* at *n*; and *d r* parallel to *a b*, cutting *m n* at *r*. Join *o r*, and produce it to meet *i l* at *q*; make I Q equal to *i q*; join F Q, and produce F Q to K. Through G, draw K L, perpendicular to K Q; through I, draw I Z, parallel to K Q, cutting K L at Z; make Z Z, equal to *a o*, and join K Z. Then produce K Z, to L, and draw A L L, parallel to Z Z.

To find the Face Mould.

Draw L A perpendicular to K L; make L A equal to L A, Z I equal Z I, and join A I. Then A I, will form the part of the face mould represented by I A, on the plan. Draw K F perpendicular to K L, and make K F equal to K F. Draw G G parallel to Z Z, cutting K L at G, and join G F. Again draw H U parallel to Z Z, and cutting K L at U; draw U H perpendicular to K L, and make U H equal to U H. Draw H E parallel to G F, and F E parallel to G H; then E F G H, will form the part of the face mould corresponding to the straight part E F G H on the plan. The intermediate points of the face mould, which form curves of the outside and inside of the rail, are thus found. Through any point C, in the convex side of the plan, draw C Y, parallel to Z Z, cutting K L at Y; and in the concave side of the plan at T, draw Y C, perpendicular to K L; and in Y C, make Y T equal to Y T, and Y C equal to Y C. Then T, is a point in the concave side, and C, a point in the convex side of the face mould. A sufficient number of points being thus found, the curved parts of the face mould may be drawn by hand, or by a slip of wood bent to the curve. No. 5, exhibits a face mould for the upper half of the rail, which is constructed in the same manner with the one just described.

How to apply the Face Mould to the Plank.

Let *a b i g*, No. 4, be the figure of the face mould, placed in due position to the pitch line K L, as when traced from the plan. X, represents the upper side, Y, the edge, and Z, the under side of the plank, from which the rail is to be taken. Draw *g* L, perpendicular to the outside of the plank. Make the angle *g* L K, on the edge of the plank, equal to the angle K L L, No. 3; and the angle *g* L K, on the under side of the plank, equal to the angle G Z I, No. 3. Make *g* L, equal to L K, and draw the chord *g i*, in the plane Z, parallel to the arris line; and then apply the points *g* and *i*, of the face mould, to the line as exhibited in the figure, and draw the form of the face mould.

Fig. 2, exhibits the section of a hand rail, drawn one-half of the full size. On B, with the radius B A, describe the half circle C A D, and divide it into

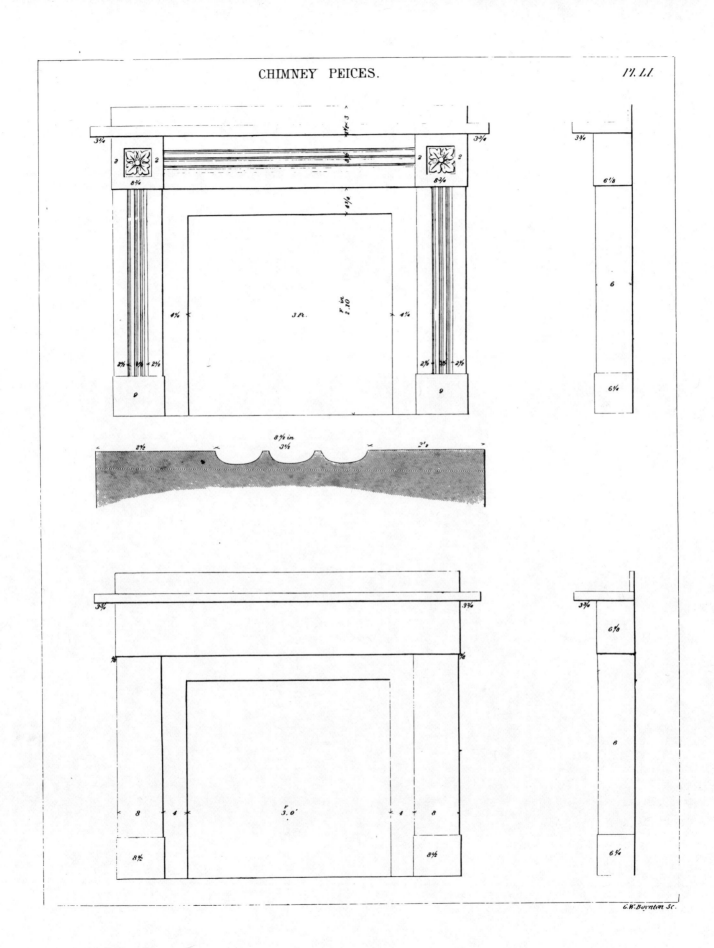

three equal parts. Draw B 1, and B 2; divide A B, into four equal parts; draw 3 *i*, parallel to D C, and cutting B 2, at *i*; draw *i l*, parallel to B I, and equal to one and one-half of the four divisions between A and B; on *i*, with the radius *i* 2, describe 2 *m*; and on *l*, with the radius *l m*, describe *m n*, and draw *n o*.

CHIMNEY-PIECES.

PLATES LI. AND LII.

A fire-place is necessary in all apartments where artificial heat is required; but the size varies according to the quantity of heat required, and the kind of fuel which is used. In a common sized room, of sixteen by nineteen feet, which is to be heated with wood, the distance between the jambs should be about three feet four inches, by two feet eight inches in height; if heated by bituminous coal, the distance should be three feet two inches, by two feet eight inches in height; and three feet by three feet, if the room is heated with anthracite coal. As much less smoke is produced by anthracite coal than by other kinds of fuel in common use, it will be well to profit by that circumstance, in extending the height of the fire-place, so that a greater portion of the heat may pass into the room.

The chimney-piece, or the finish about the fire-place, should be adapted to the use and convenience, and be made to accord with the architectural finish, of the apartment in which it is located. Care should be taken that the pilasters do not project much in front of a line with the jambs, because any considerable projection of this kind will obstruct the hot air in its passage into the room. For this reason columns are objectionable. They are also objectionable on other accounts. Two columns standing at a distance of eight diameters from each other, cannot be considered beautiful or in good taste; particularly, when we consider that their diameter will not exceed six inches, which renders all the mouldings small and indistinct, and destroys the expression which the orders bear when executed on an extended scale. They also diminish the breadth of the room, in that part of it which is most useful; for, if a table be placed in the room, it occupies the part before the fire, and so too do those who are sitting by the fire. Thus nothing is gained by the use of columns, while much is lost. In forming pilasters for a chimney-piece, make that edge which joins the jamb, project one and a quarter inches, and the other edges, six inches, by receding the breast of the chimney to a projection of ten inches from the wall, instead of the usual projection of sixteen inches. By this expedient, the shelf will be ten inches in width, four inches of which will project over the frieze, and six, lay upon the projection of the fire-place.

It is common in this part of the country, for gentlemen who build houses for their own occupation, to select such chimney-pieces as suit their own fancy; and their choice often falls upon those which most abound in finery, such as different colors of marble, the addition of a tablet to the frieze, and a profusion of unmeaning mouldings on both tablet and frieze.

It should be recollected, that the largest piece of marble which can be placed in a chimney-piece is of but small dimensions, and that, if of good proportions and well wrought, it is beautiful in itself, and should be decorated with a sparing hand. What is called decoration, ceases to be such when misplaced. Decoration is subordinate in the composition, and should be made for the place which it is to occupy, and not the place for the decoration.

On Plates LI. and LII., are four designs for chimney-pieces, which may be wrought in marble, wood, or any other material desired. If made of wood, it will be well to paint them black, in imitation of marble of that color. In this case, let the paint be properly rubbed down and nicely varnished, and a good imitation will be produced.

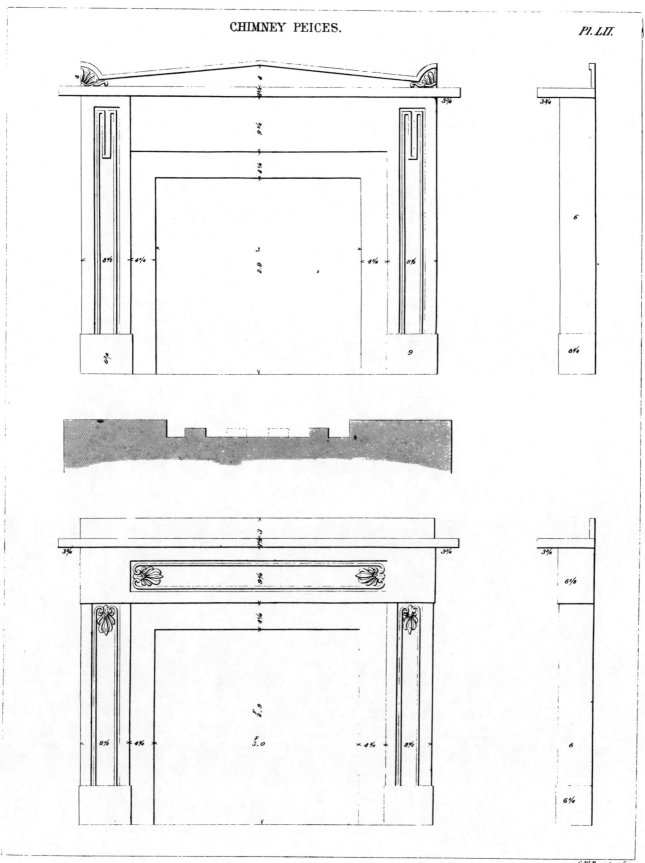

Pl. LIII.

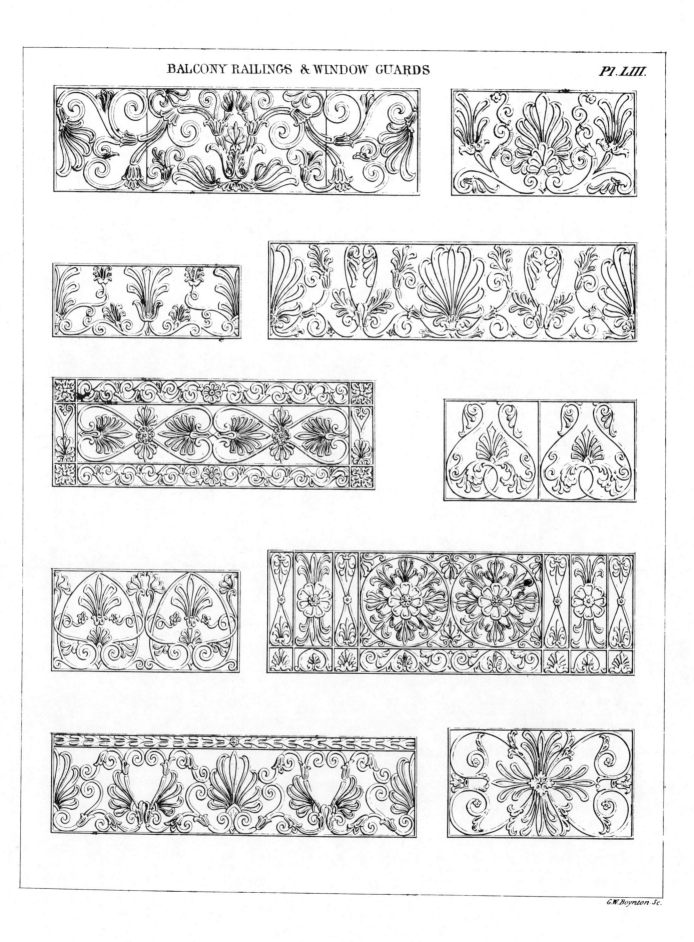

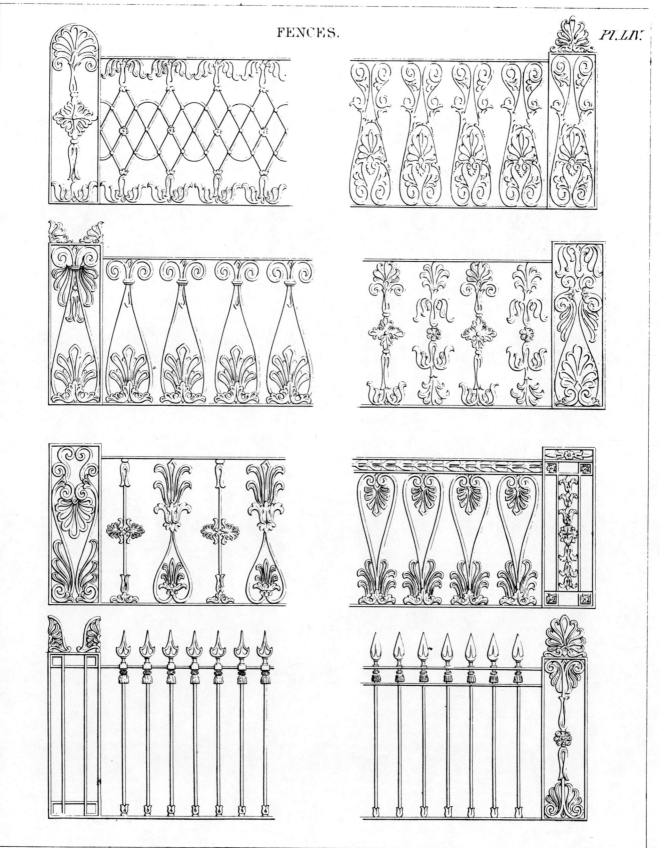

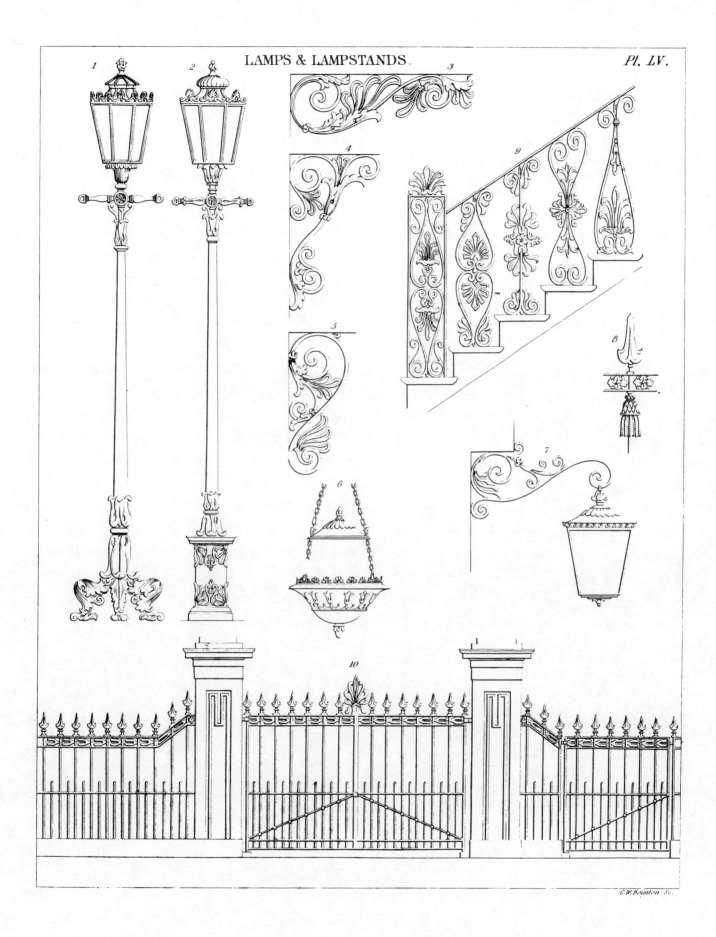

C.W.Boynton Sc.

CAST IRON.

Plates LIII., LIV., LV., LVI.

A few Plates may be usefully employed, we presume, upon this subject. The fact, that cast iron is produced in most parts of this country, and at a cost so low as to place it within the reach of all, the great amount of its yearly consumption, and the facility with which it may be wrought into the most beautiful shapes, render it an object worthy of attention here. We have accordingly given examples of balconies, railings, window guard irons, stair railings, lamps, and lamp stands, brackets, gates, verandas, and many other examples, comprising the numerous and diversified figures required in common practice. Pains have been taken to arrange and classify the numerous figures into convenient groups, so that no section shall exceed a proper size for one casting, and to join sections in such places that their appearance or stability will not be injured.

VERANDAS.

Plate LV.

This Plate contains two designs for verandas, drawn on a scale of one-fourth of an inch to a foot. They may be made either of cast, or malleable iron.

48

VASES.

Plate LVII.

On this Plate are five different designs for vases, the details of which have been carefully selected from the best antique examples, making such deviations in their form and arrangement, as was supposed would best adapt them to the practice of the day. It is believed that their forms possess a simple elegance, which they will retain, though their ornaments, from motives of economy or taste, should be omitted. The height and projection of the different members are figured in parts.

When used for the termination of pedestals and the like, their large diameter should not exceed that of the die of the pedestal, nor be less than three-fourths of it.

CHURCHES.

Plates LVIII., LIX.

On these Plates are exhibited plans and elevations of a church, which measures fifty-four feet in front, and eighty-four feet in flank. It contains, on the first and gallery floors, one hundred and sixteen pews, in which about eight hundred persons may be comfortably seated. Should it be desirable to reduce the front to fifty feet, this may be done without marring the symmetry of the building, by shortening each pew one foot. The upper and lower tiers of windows are inclosed by the same architrave, leaving the space which separates the lower from the upper tier, recessed back six inches from the face of the architrave. By this expedient, the awkward appearance pro-

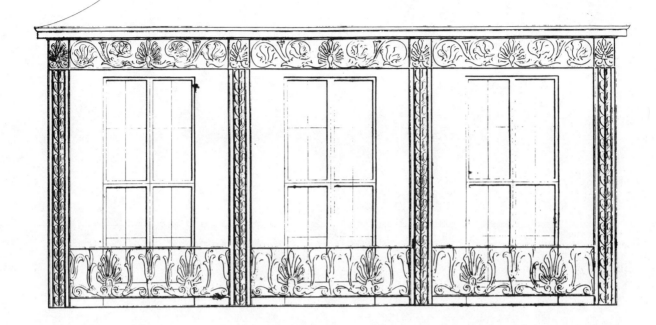

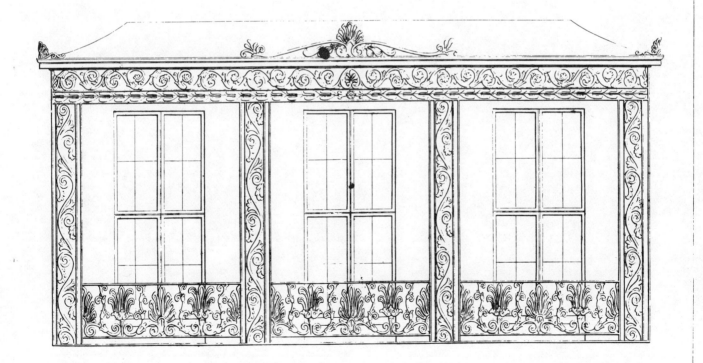

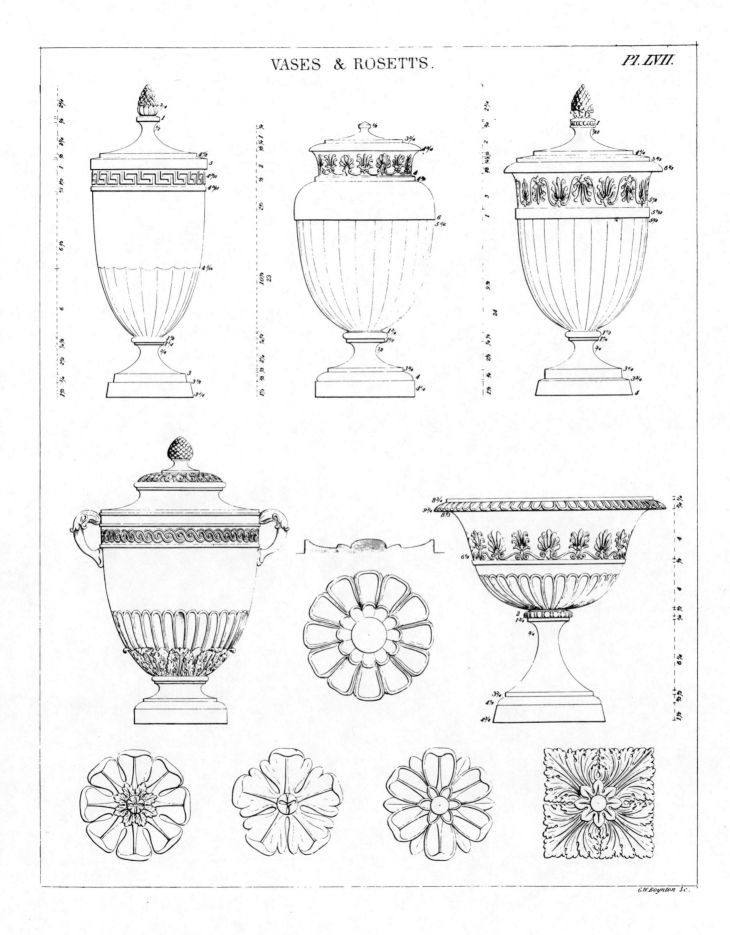

G.W.Boynton Sc.

PLAN FOR A CHURCH.

Pl. LVIII.

Gallery.

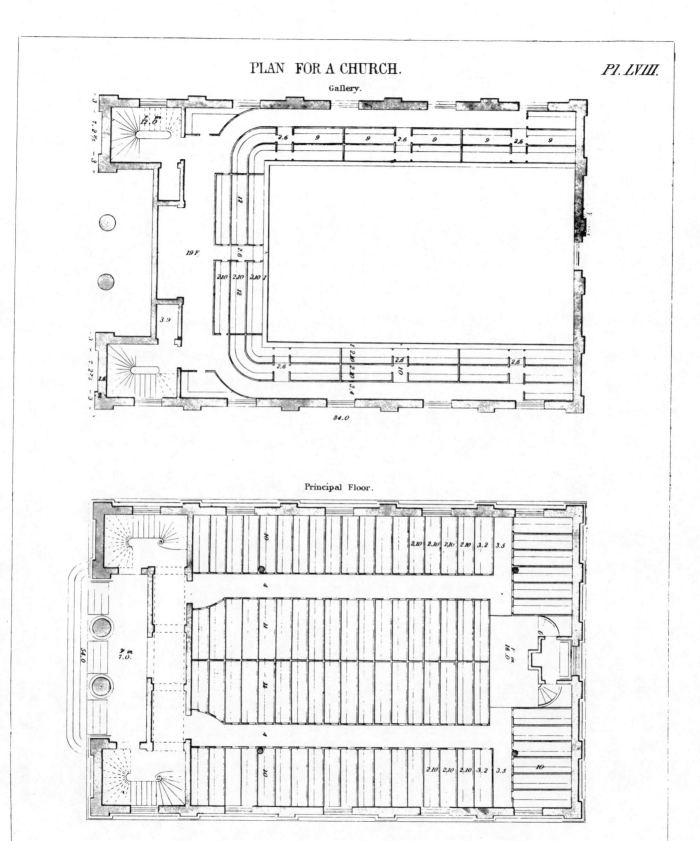

Principal Floor.

Scale of Feet

G.W.Boynton Sc.

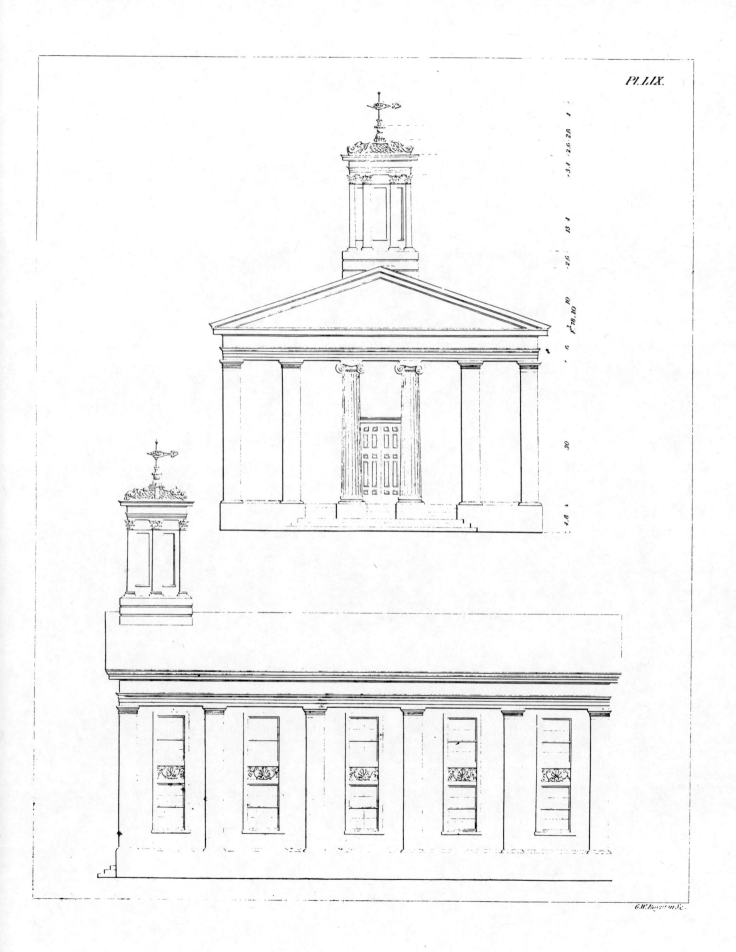

Pl. LIX.

G.W. Barton Sc.

Pl. LX.

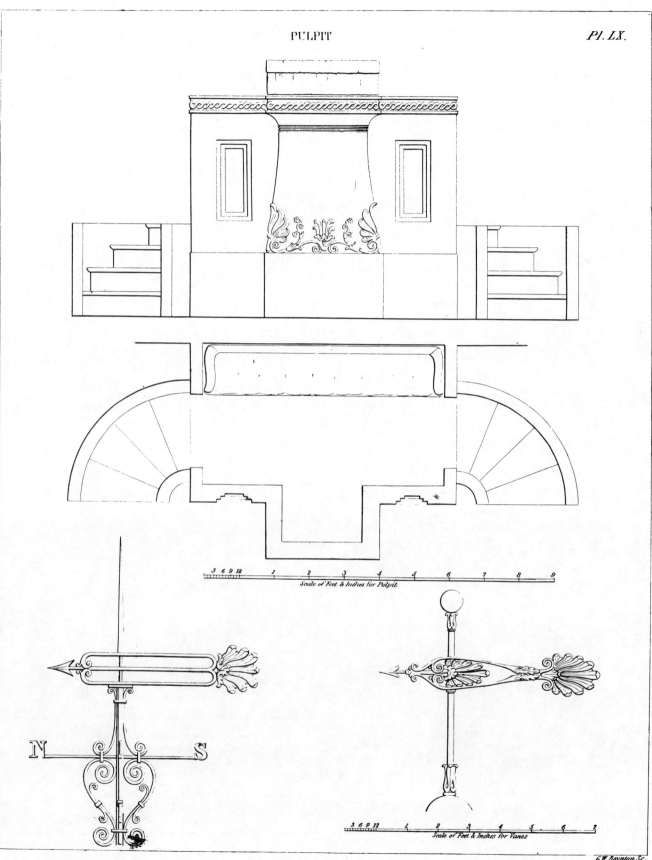

Scale of Feet & Inches for Pulpit

N   S

Scale of Feet & Inches for Vanes

G.W. Boynton Sc.

DETAILS OF A PEW.

Pl. LXI.

No.1.

No.2.

No.3.

No.4.   1   2   3   4   5   6

No.5.

No.6.

No.7.

duced by the gallery passing across the centre of the windows, is avoided, while the correct proportion of their external appearance is preserved. The expression produced by the simple massive forms composing these elevations will be in accordance with those devotional feelings, which will naturally arise, in a building-devoted to the worship of the Supreme Being. It is intended that the interior finish of the building should accord with the exterior. The ceiling may be gently curved upwards, and divided into deep sunken panels. The ceiling under the galleries must be ten feet high from the floor at the front, and incline upwards toward the wall, so as to leave a sufficient space for the architrave to pass over the windows. That part of the front of the galleries, which is between the columns, may be trussed with iron trusses, in the same manner as is shown on Plate LXV. On Plate LX., are a plan and elevation of a pulpit suitable for this building.

PEWS, &c.

Plate LXI.

Figs. 1, 2, and 3, are three examples of block ornaments, intended to be placed where the architraves abutt, at the angles of the doors and windows. The centres of the elevations of each are respectively decorated with a honey-suckle, and a sculptured and a turned rosette. No. 4, represents a section of the latter block and turned rosette, drawn at full size. No. 7, represents an end elevation of two pews, showing the paneling and capping on the doors and piers. The dotted lines show the places, on the opposite side of this elevation, where the risers, the seats, and the partition between the pews are situated. This elevation is drawn on a scale of one inch to a foot. No. 5, shows a section of the capping on the doors; No. 6, the capping on the partition between the pews, drawn full size for practice.

13

THEORY AND PRACTICE OF CARPENTRY.

Plate LXII.

By the theory of carpentry, the artisan is taught the nature, quality, strength, and stiffness of those materials, which he is obliged to use in the course of his occupation, also the numerous and complicated strains, to which they are exposed, and the remedies, by which these strains can be effectually overcome. It is therefore of great importance to the practical carpenter, that he acquire a sufficient knowledge of this science, to enable him to give the due proportions of the various pieces of timber and other materials which compose the roofs and other parts of buildings. This information is furnished by the results of various experiments, made for the purpose of ascertaining the different strains which different sizes of those materials can bear, by several scientific gentlemen of Europe. Of course, these experiments were made on European timber. We therefore must make proper allowances for the difference of timber. Different individuals have arrived at different results in their experiments. We cannot, therefore, put implicit confidence in any of them; but taking them collectively, and making proper allowances for difference in timber, we may assist our judgment and obtain correct views on the subject.

The principal strains to which timbers and other materials are exposed, are the following:

First, that strain by which a beam is drawn in the direction of its length. The strength by which the beam resists this strain, is called its cohesion. The experiment, by which the cohesive power of a beam or stick of known dimensions is ascertained, is easily performed in the following manner. The stick is suspended vertically by one extremity, and to the lower extremity are attached weights, which, being increased until the stick breaks, thus determine its cohesive power. To this strain, king posts, tie beams, &c. are liable.

The second strain, is when the load tends to compress the beam in the direction of its length. To this strain, truss beams, pillars, struts, &c. are exposed.

The third strain, is when the load tends to break the beam across. This is called a cross or transverse strain. To this strain all kinds of bearing timbers are liable.

The following list, which gives the cohesive strength of several beams and bars, an inch square, is taken from one made by Mr. Emerson. The rod of cast iron is taken from the experiments of Rennie. The amount placed opposite each kind, expresses its cohesive strength, or the weight which will be required to break it, when drawn in the direction of its length.

Iron Rod, an inch square, will bear, ...	76,400	pounds.
Cast Iron, " "	18,656	"
Brass, " "	35,600	"
Hempen Rope, " "	19,600	"
Ivory, " "	15,700	"
Oak, Box and Plum-tree, "	7,850	"
Elm, Ash and Beech, "	6,070	"
Walnut and Plum, "	5,360	"
Red Fir, Holley and Crab, "	5,000	"
Cherry and Hazel, "	4,760	"
Alder, Asp, Birch and Willow, "	4,290	"
Lead, "	430	"

It is also given as a practical rule by Mr. Emerson, that a cylinder whose diameter is six inches, will carry, when loaded to one-fourth of its absolute strength, as follows. Iron, 135 cwt.; Good Rope, 22 cwt.; Oak, 14 cwt.; Fir, 9 cwt.

By these experiments we see what an immense load a rod of one inch square is capable of suspending. And we likewise see that this strain is not likely to be overrated in practice.

Suppose it required to know the weight that an oak joist, of three by four inches, will sustain. Multiply the depth by the breadth of the joist in inches;

and that product, which is twelve, by the number of pounds set against oak in the table, 7,850. The product, 94,200 pounds, is the answer.

We now come to the second strain, that of compression in the direction of the length. But few experiments on this strain have been made, and the results of those few do not agree. It is maintained by some writers that the resistance to compression is about equal to that of extension; but the experiments of Du Hamel on cross strain, seem to prove that the resistance to compression is not more than two-thirds of that to extension. It is however fortunate for the practical workman, that this strain is not often overrated; for it rarely happens in practice that a body employed to sustain a heavy load is found insufficient for that purpose.

According to Mr. Rondelet's experiments on cubic inches of oak, it required from 5,000 to 6,000 pounds to crush a piece of that size; and under this pressure its length was reduced more than one-third.

Mr. Rennie's experiments produced results considerably lower. A cubic inch of elm was crushed by 1,284 pounds; American pine, by 1,606 pounds; and English oak, by 3,860 pounds.

We now come to the cross strain, to which all bearing beams, joists, &c. are liable. The resistance to this strain is much less than that of either of the others.

A Table of the Cross or Transverse Strain of different kinds of Wood, each Piece being one foot long, one inch broad, and one inch deep.

Oak, ...	660 pounds.
Ash, ...	635 "
Beech, ...	677 "
Elm, ...	540 "
Walnut, green, ...	487 "
Spruce, American, ...	570 "
Hard Pine, do.	658 "
Birch, ...	517 "
Poplar, Lombard, ...	327 "
Chestnut, ...	450 "

The above table is selected from Tredgold's Carpentry. It expresses the breaking weight of each piece. It will not, therefore, be proper to permanently load either of the pieces with more than one-half of the breaking weight. The effect of this strain produces, on the upper part of the beam, a compression in the direction of its length; and on the under part, an extension in the direction of its length. To illustrate this subject more fully, I will here introduce some of Du Hamel's experiments on the stiffness of beams, the results of which ought to be well understood.

Du Hamel took six bars of willow, three feet long and one and one-half inches square. After suitable experiments, he found that they were broken by 525 pounds, on an average. Six bars were next cut through with a saw, one-third of the depth from the upper surface, and each cut was filled with a wedge of dry oak, inserted with a little force. These were broken by 551 pounds, on an average. Six other bars were broken through by 542 pounds, on an average, after being cut half through and filled up in a similar manner. Six other bars were cut three-fourths through, and broken by the pressure of 530 pounds, on an average. A baton was then cut three-fourths through, and loaded until nearly broken. It was then unloaded, and a thicker wedge was introduced tightly into the cut, so as to straighten the bar by filling up the space left by the compression of the wood. In this state the bar was broken by 577 pounds.

From these experiments, we perceive that more than two-thirds of the thickness of a beam contributes nothing to its strength. And here we also see, that the compressibility of this kind of strain appears much greater than its dilatability, which circumstance greatly increases its power of withstanding a transverse strain.

We see likewise that gains may be cut from the upper surface of a beam downwards, to one-third or one-half of the depth, and joists inserted tightly therein, without reducing the strength of the beam. Observe, however, that the size of the joists is not reduced by shrinkage. It is worthy of remark, that in all the experiments made for ascertaining the resistance to pressure,

14

the strength of the beam is found to be as the breadth and square of the depth directly, and inversely as the length. The strength of a beam therefore depends chiefly on its depth, or rather on that dimension which is in the direction of the strain. If a beam two inches deep and one broad, support a given weight, another beam of the same depth and double the breadth will support double the weight. But if a beam two inches deep and one inch broad, support a given weight, another of four inches deep and one inch broad will support four times the weight. Hence, beams of equal breadths are to each other as the square of their depths. Again, if a beam of a given cross section and one foot long support a known weight, another beam of the same cross section but two feet long will support only half the known weight.

Buffon's experiments, which were made on large scantlings, and were therefore free from those irregularities unavoidable on small specimens, would seem to show that the strength diminishes in a ratio greater than the inverse proportion of the length. Both reason and experience seem to confirm the truth of these experiments.

A simple arithmetical rule, derived from these experiments, is therefore given, by which the breaking weight of any scantling, the breadth, depth and length being given, may be known. Divide the breaking weight by the length in feet; subtract 10 from the quotient; multiply the remainder by the breadth, and that product by the square of the depth, both expressed in inches. The result is the greatest load in pounds.

For example. Required the resistance of a spruce joist, 17 feet long, 12 inches in depth, and 2 inches in breadth. The breaking weight placed against spruce in the above list is 570. Divide 570 by 17, the length in feet, and you have 33 for the quotient, nearly. Subtract 10 from 33, and the remainder is 23. This remainder being multiplied by 2, the breadth in inches, the product is 46. Multiply this product by 144, the square of the depth in inches, (the square of any number being obtained by multiplying it by itself,) and you have 6,624 for the answer. I have left out the fractions in the above operation, knowing that any deviation which makes the result smaller, is on the safe side.

Ans. 6,624.

Required the resistance of a hard pine beam, 20 feet long, 12 inches in depth, and 10 inches in breadth. *Ans.* 31,680.

We must recollect, that all the experiments, from which the above results are obtained, were made on wood of the most perfect kind, free from knots, shakes, spots, or rot, and not cross-grained, &c. Every practical workman knows, that in roofs, floors, or any other piece of framing of any considerable magnitude, such perfection in timber cannot be expected. It will be wise in him, therefore, to make all due allowance for imperfections in timber.

If a floor of a dwelling-house be loaded with people, to which it is always liable, the load is then equal to one hundred and twenty pounds on each square foot; we therefore see that the floor of a room of twenty by seventeen feet, must be capable of resisting a pressure of 40,800 pounds.

The bearing weight of one of these joists (supposing them to be of spruce) is obtained as follows. The breaking weight of spruce is 570. Divide 570 by the length of the joist, which is 17 feet, and you obtain 33 feet, nearly, (for I leave out the decimals.) Deduct 10 from 33, and the remainder is 23. Multiply 23 by 2, the breadth of the joist, and you obtain 46. Multiply 46 by the square of the depth of the joist, which is 144, and you obtain 6,624, which is the breaking weight; and the breaking weight of the 20 joists, collectively, which are in the floor (I call each of the trimmers equal to two common joists) is 132,480 pounds. And they contain 680 feet of timber, board measure.

We will now see, in the same manner, what the resistance to pressure is, of a floor framed in the common way, with a beam lying longitudinally through the centre of the room, twelve inches square, and filled up on each side with joists four by four inches. The breaking weight of the beam, if of spruce, is 31,104 pounds. In this calculation, I do not allow any diminution in the strength of the beam, on account of the gains cut into it, because if the joists are tightly pressed into the gains and prevented from shrinking, the beam will not be weakened. 31,104 pounds is one-half of the ultimate strength of the floor. Double this sum, and you have 62,208 for the ultimate strength of the whole floor. It requires 602 feet of timber, board measure, to complete this floor. By this calculation, we see, that with the same quantity of timber in the wide joist floor, we have more than double the strength that is obtained by a beam and joist floor.

If a church be made of wood, and without a gallery, it is common to frame the sides with a girt, placed about midway between the plate and the sill. The posts and girts in this case cannot be less than ten inches, and the studs four by four inches. Let us suppose a building, fifty feet long and twenty-five high, to be framed in this way. The mortice made in the middle of the post cannot be less than two inches, and the pin-holes, which pass through the tenon of each girt, than two inches more. The tenon and pin-holes reduce the solid part of the post to eight inches, and even less; for, in taking the square of the depth, it must be taken in two parts; first, from the face of the post to the mortice, two inches, the square of which is four, and the remaining part of the post beyond the mortice is six inches, the square of which is thirty-six, which with the four added makes forty; whereas the square of eight is sixty-four.

If these posts be of spruce, the bearing weight of each will be 3,840, and collectively 15,360. Double this sum, and we have 30,720 pounds, which is the ultimate resistance to any strain to which the whole side of the house is liable. The greatest force produced by the wind on a vertical wall is equal to forty pounds on a square foot. It will therefore be unsafe not to afford a resistance fully adequate to overcome that strain. The posts, girts and studs, will contain 2,083 feet, board measure. We will now suppose this facade to be framed with spruce studs, twenty-five feet long, two inches thick, and eight inches deep. The breaking weight of one is 1,944, and of thirty-seven, the number required to complete the side, 71,928 pounds, which is the ultimate strength of the whole side; and they contain altogether 1,354 feet, board measure.

These principles may, with great advantage, be applied to all framed houses, whether large or small.

Suppose it be required to execute the frame of a common sized house, two stories in height, the studs ten feet long, the sills, plates and posts, each seven inches square, and the girt seven inches thick and twelve inches wide, which width seems to be required on account of the floor being of the same depth. We will now suppose the studs to be two inches thick and seven wide, instead of four by four inches, the common size. It is manifest that studs are not liable to any strain, in the direction parallel to the side of the building on which they are situated. Two inches is therefore quite a sufficient thickness, in that respect; and so is any other thickness, which is capable of receiving and retaining the nails, by which the outside covering is fastened to the studs. When the studs are short and the building small, the thickness may be reduced one and a half inches; but, in this case, care should be used in driving the nails into the studs; for, if they be driven in a straight line, the stud will be liable to crack, and weaken the hold of the nails. The breadth of the stud being the same as. that of the girts and plates, the two latter rest firmly on the heads of the studs, and are thus prevented from canting or settling; but if the studs were of the usual size, say four by four inches, the girt would project three inches over them, and this being in the place where the joists are tenoned into the floor, the whole weight of the floor would of course be thrown upon this unsupported part of the girt, and a settlement inevitably caused on that edge. A stud two inches thick, seven inches wide, and ten feet long, will resist a pressure of four thousand and eight pounds, making a difference of more than one-third in favor of the two by seven inch studs.

If one and a half inches should be thought a sufficient thickness to retain the nails of the outside covering, it would resist a pressure of three thousand, four hundred and fifty-two pounds. The width of the studs may be reduced, and still be amply strong; for, since the greatest pressure on the vertical side of a wall is forty pounds to each cubic foot, studs ten feet long, placed eighteen inches from each other, would sustain a pressure of six hundred pounds.

As the girts are not liable to any other strain than that caused by the

15

pressure of the floor downwards, and by the wind from without, which is abundantly resisted by the floor, they may be reduced to six inches. If the stud is made one and a half by six inches, it will sustain a pressure of two thousand, five hundred and thirty-eight pounds.

I now leave this subject, trusting that enough has been shown respecting these calculations, to convince every one of the great advantage to be derived by putting them into practice.

PLATE LXII.

Fig. 1, exhibits an example of a truss simply constructed for a roof of thirty feet span. I shall describe the different strains to which this truss is liable, and the best means of resisting them.

If a load be laid on the rafters of this truss, it is evident that the downward pressure will cause the heads of the rafters to press hard against the king post, and the lower ends to press equally hard against the abutment at each end of the tie beam. The rafters are thus strained by a compression in the direction of their length; and if no other strain were to be resisted, a stick of timber of small dimensions would be sufficient. But it is evident that a cross strain is also to be provided for. The latter strain must be resisted by struts, and by making the rafter of a size equal to the resistance of that strain. The pressure of the rafters against the abutment, at each end of the tie beam, causes that beam to be strained by an extension in the direction of its length; and, moreover, the load laid upon this beam, and the weight of the ceiling which is suspended from the under surface, produce a cross strain, which must be resisted by suspending this beam by the king post, and by making it, as in the case of the rafters, of sufficient size to resist the pressure.

The strain in the king post is an extension in the direction of its length. A small piece of timber is therefore adequate to resist that strain; for we have seen that an oak joist of three by four inches is capable of suspending 94,200 pounds. The pressure of the rafters against the head of the post

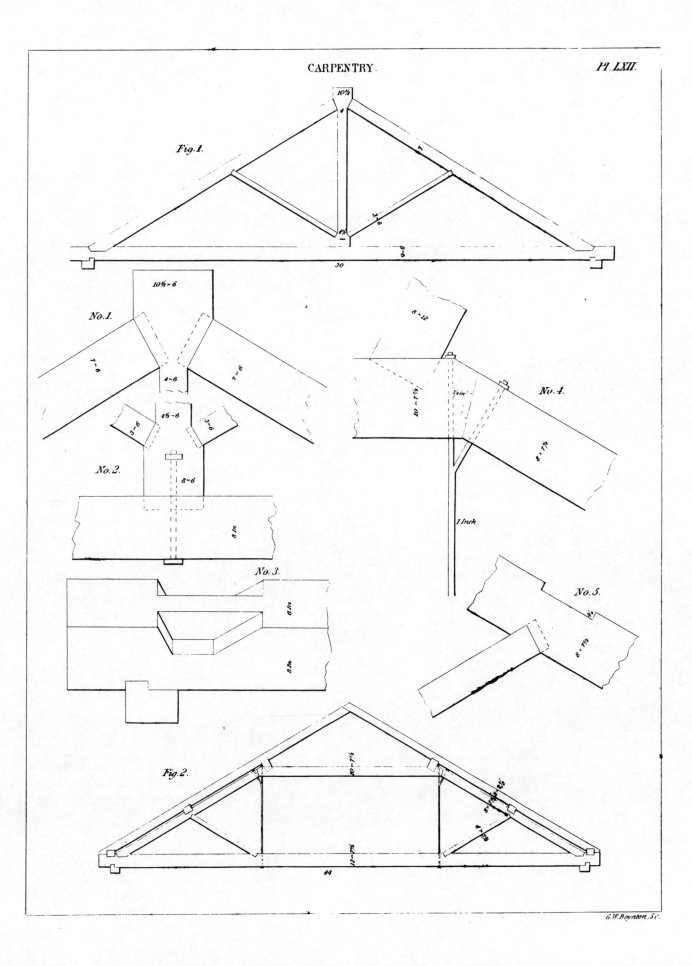

Fig. 1.

No. 1.

No. 2.

No. 3.

No. 4.

No. 5.

Fig. 2.

being very great, they will be apt to indent themselves into it, and cause a small settlement of the roof, unless the post be made of hard wood. But let it be observed, moreover, that this part of the king post should be made as small as the strain on it will admit; otherwise the shrinkage of the post will produce the same effect as the indentation of the rafters. The strain on the strut is wholly that of a compression in the direction of its length, which a small piece of timber will be able to resist.

No. 1, represents the heads of the king post and rafters, and their connection with each other. The dotted lines show the tenon, which should be just long enough to steady the heads of the rafters. No. 2, shows the foot of the king post and struts, also a side elevation of the tie beam, and the bolt which connects the tie beam to the king post. No. 3, shows the end of the tie beam, and the method of its connection with the foot of the rafters, also a section of the plate framed into the tie beam.

It is to be remembered, that all bearing joints must be made at right angles with the strain, or in other words, with the upper side of the rafters.

Fig. 2, is an example of a section of a roof, with iron queen posts, placed at such a distance from each other, as to render the space between them useful for lodging rooms, or such other purposes as may be desirable. By using that material for the queen post, instead of wood, the shrinkage of the head of the post, and the indentation of the rafters in the same are avoided. The additional expense cannot be an objection to substituting iron for wood, as it will not in any important roof be at all proportional to the advantage to be gained.

Fig. 4, shows the junction and connection of the head of the rafter with the end of the straining beam, and also a section of the purloin, which is notched down upon the straining beam, as is shown by the dotted lines. It shows also the head of the iron queen post, the dotted lines representing one branch of it passing through the rafter, and the other branch passing through the end of the straining beam. Fig. 5, shows the method of connecting the strut to the rafter, and the manner of notching the rafter to receive the purloin.

The above details are figured in inches, and are drawn on a scale of one inch to a foot.

Plate LXIII.

This Plate exhibits an example of a roof, whose tie beam is forty-four feet in bearing. The queen posts are proposed to be made of wood, their smallest dimensions being six inches in front, and eight in flank. This size is sufficient to resist the greatest strain that can ever be thrown upon them, though they be made of soft pine. If made of hard pine, or any other wood equally hard and strong, their size may be reduced to five inches in front, with the same measure in flank. It will be wise to reduce the heads of these posts to the smallest dimensions which the strain to which they are exposed will admit, in order to render the shrinkage as small as possible.

No. 1, shows the connection of the tie beam, the principal and small rafters, and the iron strap at the foot of the principal rafter. No. 2, shows a section of the purloin, and the manner of notching it to the principal rafter, and the notching the small rafter to the purloin, also the connection of the strut with the principal rafter. No. 3, exhibits the head of the queen post and of the principal rafter, showing also the end of the straining beam and a section of the purloin, with the small rafter notched upon it. No. 4, shows the tie beam, the foot of the king post and strut, and the method of their connection with each other. All these details are correctly drawn on a scale of one-half inch to a foot, and figured in inches. Fig. 2, exhibits a section of a roof, in which the trusses, for the support of the small rafters, are placed at right angles with the pitch. By this method of framing, a larger space under the rafters is rendered useful, and the roof is constructed with more economy, while it is equally safe, when the trusses do not exceed thirty feet bearing. I have extended the trusses to fifty feet with perfect safety; but in this case they were made deeper, and four struts were used instead of two.—*a*, and *a*, show the sections of the lower truss beams, each of which forms a timber

Pl. LXIII.

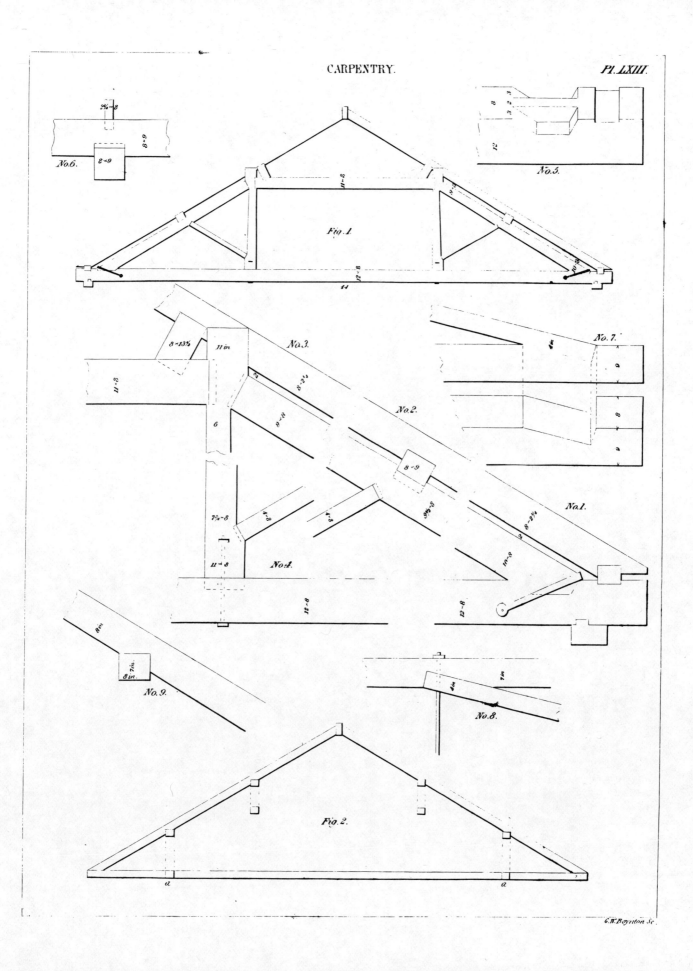

G.W.Boynton Sc.

in the floor. No. 7, shows the method of connecting the end of the beam with that of the strut; and No. 8, the upper end of the strut, with the upper truss beam. No. 9, shows a section of the upper truss beam, and its connection with the rafter.

Nos. 10, and 11, on Plate LXV., show elevations of the trusses, when complete, and may with propriety be called trussed purloins. Fig. 1, exhibits a simple method of framing floors. This is supposed to be the floor of one of two parlors, which are connected by sliding doors, and are seventeen feet in width, and twenty feet in length. The timber *a*, is supposed to be under the sliding doors; and *b b*, represent two courses of stiffeners, which must be fitted in with some force, taking care that those adjoining the wall are not forced so as to press the wall out of its place. No. 2, shows a side view of a joist or beam, and the manner of proportioning and forming the tenon. It is often necessary to floor over apartments, whose great extent renders the common flooring insufficient. I have therefore given here an example of a floor, the joists of which are thirty feet bearing. This is fully adequate to sustain any pressure to which it may be liable, and by increasing the means here shown, it may be extended to forty feet bearing, with perfect safety. Fig. 3, exhibits a plan for this floor, showing four joists, two inches thick, and thirteen inches deep.—*a a*, and *a a*, near each end of the joists, show two iron bars, two and a half inches wide, and three-fourths of an inch thick, let down into the joists, the iron trusses passing through them midway between each two of the joists. These trusses are three-fourths of an inch square, and pass under the two ties *b b*, and *b b*, and are strained up by turning a nut at each end. The ties *b b* and *b b*, must be sufficiently thick to be notched up on each side of the joists, so as to prevent them from vibrating when the truss is strained up; and it will also be necessary to put on stiffeners at *f, f, f*, and *f*, for the same purpose. No. 4, exhibits a side view of a joist, with a side view of the truss which passes under the ties at *c*, and *c*, and also the manner of cutting in the iron bars, near the ends of the joists, at *a a*, and *a a*. No. 5, shows the screw and nut at the end of the truss, on a large scale.

16

If this floor is used for common purposes, not more than one-third, or, at most, one-half of the trusses here shown, will be required to render it sufficiently strong; for we must consider, that the strain on the truss is an extension in the direction of its length, and therefore it is capable of sustaining an immense weight. One course of the floor boards, directly over the ends of trusses, had best be put down with wood screws, in order that it may be easily removed, if it should be rendered necessary by an extension of the trusses; in which case, the floor may be raised by turning the nuts at each end of the trusses.

CARPENTRY.

Plate LXIV.

This Plate exhibits an example of a roof, with inclined tie beams, so arranged, as to admit an arched ceiling to rise up within it. Though this kind of roof is frequently employed, when necessity or economy make it desirable to extend the ceiling up into the roof, yet it will be wise to avoid its use, whenever this can be conveniently done, since its form is such as to throw a great strain upon the tie beams and king posts, thus requiring these timbers to be very much increased in size, over those of the common roof, which causes a greater proportion of shrinkage and indentation of the timbers, where they are connected, and of course a great and sometimes fearful settling of the roof.

Fig. 1, shows an elevation of one pair of rafters, and the manner of forming and securing the iron truss around the ends of the tie beams, passing under the iron plates at *e e*, and extending up and passing over at the head of the king post at *d*. It shows also the iron strap, connected at the centre by screws, which secures the tie beams, at their junction, from sliding or settling.

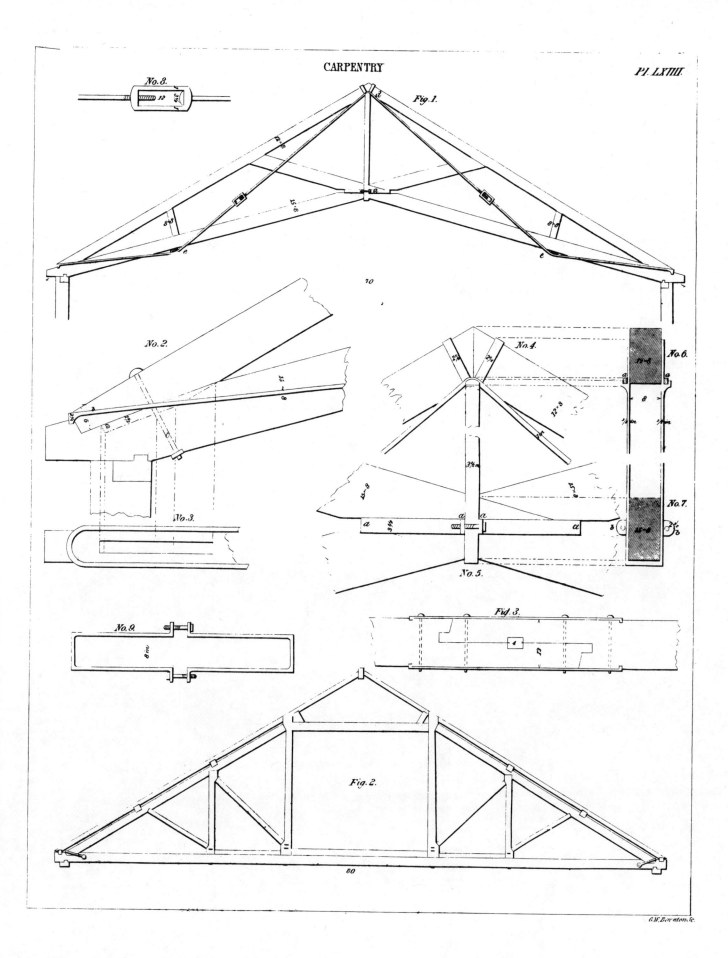

No. 8.

Fig. 1.

No. 2.

No. 3.

No. 9.

No. 4.

No. 5.

No. 6.

No. 7.

Fig. 3.

Fig. 2.

Pl. LXV.

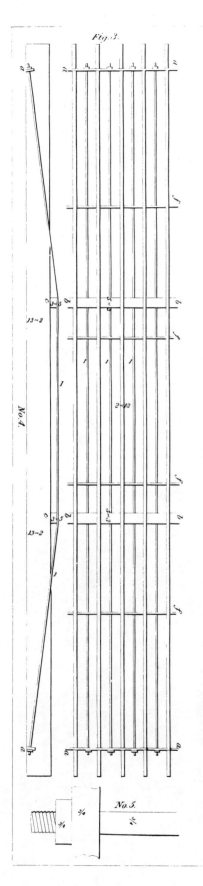

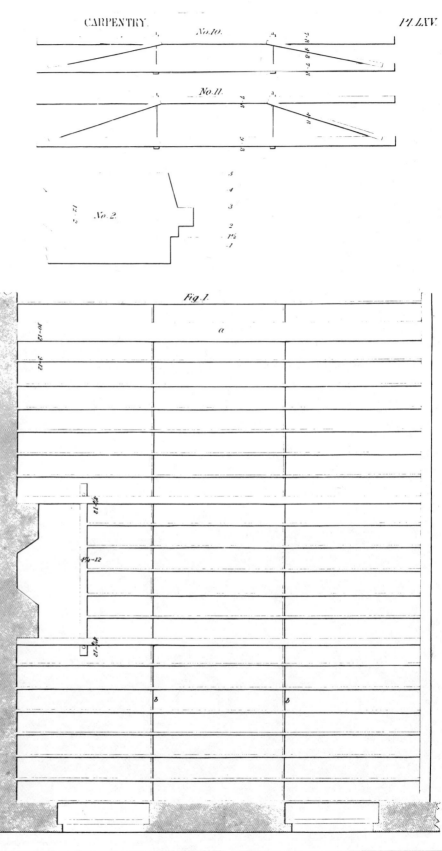

No. 2, exhibits the method of connecting the foot of the tie beam with that of the rafter ; *b*, represents the iron truss passing around the foot of the rafter ; the dotted line at *a*, shows the length of the tenon, and at *c*, the bolt by which the beam and rafter are confined to each other. No. 3, exhibits the upper surface of the beam, fitted to receive the rafter. No. 4, shows the connection of the head of the rafters with that of the king post. The rafters are intended to be butted together, for the purpose of preventing shrinkage. No. 5, shows the tie beams at their junction, and the manner of fitting the iron strap to them, (see its plan at No. 9,) which will, if proper attention is given, in setting up the screws, prevent them from settling at that place. No. 6, gives a side view of the head of the king post, and *a a*, sections of the iron truss passing over it. No. 7, gives a side view of the foot of the king post, passing under the tie beams, and *b b*, the ends of the iron strap, the same as *a a*, in No. 5. No. 8, exhibits the method of forming a wrench, by which the iron truss may be strained up, if required, either by shrinkage, or by the extension of the truss.

It should be remembered, that the strain on this roof is very great. It is therefore necessary that the materials, of which it is constructed, and the labor bestowed upon it, should be of the most perfect kind. The joints should fit perfectly in every part. The iron should be of the best quality and workmanship, and care should be taken that the threads of the screws are sufficiently large, and the nuts, which encircle them, of a proper size, not less in thickness than the diameter of the body of the screws. Let the bands, which inclose the timbers, be made somewhat thicker, at their angles, than in other parts. And lastly, if shrinkage or indentation of any of the joints of the timbers, or an extension in length of any part of the iron work, should be discovered, let them be immediately set up by the screws provided for the purpose. If these precautions be strictly observed, I have no doubt that a roof, made in imitation of this example, will stand as perfectly, and with as little settling, as those formed with a horizontal beam.

Fig. 2, is an example of a roof remarkable for its antiquity, simplicity and strength. It has been so often constructed, that it needs no explanation here. Fig. 3, exhibits a good method of scarfing timbers. It is shown sufficiently plain upon the Plate, without further explanation.

Plate LXVI.

Fig. 1, shows a method of trussing a partition between rooms, in which two doors are placed. If the floor below the partition should require support, it may be suspended by iron rods passing up through the beam at the head of the trusses. It is frequently desirable and sometimes necessary, to construct fire-proof rooms, where it is not convenient to spare the room, or incur the expense, of vaulting in the ordinary way. I have therefore extracted from Tredgold's excellent treatise on the strength of cast iron and other metals, a table furnishing the various forms and sizes of cast iron joists, from eight to twenty-four feet in length, and the manner of turning brick arches between them, so as to make the floor fire-proof. This kind of floor will not occupy more space than is required for a floor of wood, and can be constructed at a much less expense, than the vaulted floor. I have also taken from the same author, portions of other tables, giving the dimensions of various cast iron beams and columns, and the weight which they will respectively bear.

TABLE OF CAST IRON JOISTS, *for fire-proof floors, where the load is not greater than one hundred and twenty pounds to a superficial foot.*

Length of joists.	Half brick arches, breadth of beams two inches.			Nine inch arches, breadth of beams three inches.		
	Three feet span.	Four feet span.	Five feet span.	Six feet span.	Seven feet span.	Eight feet span.
Feet.	Depth in inches.	Depth in inches.	Depth in inches.	Depth in inches.	Depth in inches.	Depth in inches.
8	$4\frac{1}{2}$	$5\frac{1}{4}$	$5\frac{3}{4}$	$5\frac{1}{4}$	$5\frac{3}{4}$	6
10	$5\frac{1}{2}$	$6\frac{1}{2}$	7	$6\frac{1}{2}$	$7\frac{1}{4}$	$7\frac{1}{2}$
12	$6\frac{3}{4}$	$7\frac{3}{4}$	$8\frac{1}{2}$	$7\frac{3}{4}$	$8\frac{1}{2}$	9
14	$7\frac{3}{4}$	9	10	$9\frac{1}{4}$	10	$10\frac{1}{2}$
18	10	$11\frac{3}{4}$	$12\frac{3}{4}$	$11\frac{3}{4}$	13	$13\frac{1}{2}$
20	$11\frac{1}{4}$	13	14	13	$14\frac{1}{4}$	15
22	$12\frac{1}{4}$	$14\frac{1}{4}$	$15\frac{1}{2}$	$4\frac{1}{4}$	$15\frac{3}{4}$	$16\frac{1}{2}$
24	$13\frac{1}{4}$	$15\frac{1}{2}$	17	$15\frac{1}{2}$	17	18

Pl. LXVI.

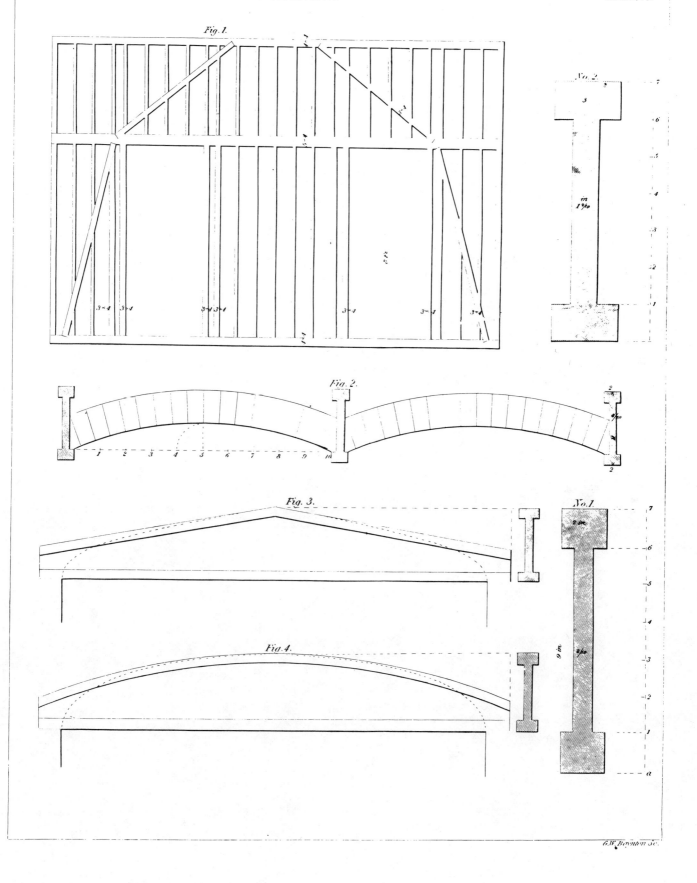

Fig. 1.

No. 2.

Fig. 2.

Fig. 3.

No. 1.

Fig. 4.

For half brick arches, the breadth of the beam No. 1, Plate LXVI., should be two inches, and the thickness of the middle, eight-tenths of an inch. The depth of *a* 1, and *b* 7, should be each one-seventh of the whole depth, which is given in the table, in inches, for each span.

For nine inch arches, the breadth of the beam No. 2, is three inches, and the breadth of the middle part, one and two-tenths inches, and the depth one-seventh, as in the other case. A beam whose upper surface is bounded by a semi-ellipsis, as shown by the dotted lines on Figs. 3 and 4, is equally strong with one which has a straight line for the upper surface. It is evident therefore, that a considerable saving in the expense of beams may be made by forming them in imitation of Figs. 3 or 4.

A TABLE, *showing the weight or pressure a Beam of Cast Iron, one inch in breadth, will sustain, without destroying its elastic force, when it is supported at the ends, and loaded in the middle of its length.*

Depths. Inches.	1 foot. Weight in lbs.	2 feet. Weight in lbs.	3 feet. Weight in lbs.	4 feet. Weight in lbs.	5 feet. Weight in lbs.	6 feet. Weight in lbs.	7 feet. Weight in lbs.	8 feet. Weight in lbs.	9 feet. Weight in lbs.	10 feet. Weight in lbs.
1	850	425	283	212	170	142	121	106	95	85
1½	1,912	956	637	477	383	320	273	239	214	192
2		1,700	1,132	848	680	568	484	425	380	340
2½		2,656	1,769	1,325	1,062	887	756	662	594	531
3			2,547	1,908	1,530	1,278	1,089	954	855	765
3½			3,467	2,597	2,082	1,739	1,482	1,298	1,164	1,041
4				3,392	2,720	2,272	1,936	1,700	1,520	1,360
4½				4,293	3,442	2,875	2,450	2,146	1,924	1,721
5					4,250	3,560	3,050	2,650	2,375	2,125
6					6,120	5,112	4,356	3,816	3,420	3,060
7						6,958	5,929	5,194	4,655	4,165
8						9,088	7,744	6,784	6,080	5,440
9							9,801	8,586	7,695	6,885
10							12,100	10,600	9,500	8,500
11								12,826	11,495	10,285
12								15,264	13,680	12,240
13									16,100	14,400
14									18,600	16.700

17

TABLE—*Of the strength of Cast Iron Beams, continued.*

Lengths....12 feet.	14 feet.	16 feet.	18 feet.	20 feet.	22 feet.	24 feet.	26 feet.	28 feet.	30 feet.
Depths. Inches. Weight in lbs.	Weight in lbs.	Weight in lbs.	Weight in lbs.	Weight in lbs.	Weight in lbs.	Weight in lbs.	Weight in lbs.	Weight in lbs.	Weight in lbs.
2 283	243	212	189	170	154	142	131	121	113
3 637	546	478	425	382	347	318	294	273	255
4 1,133	971	849	755	680	618	566	523	485	453
5 1,771	1,518	1,328	1,180	1,062	966	885	817	759	708
6 2,548	2,184	1,912	1,699	1,530	1,390	1,274	1,176	1,092	1,019
7 3,471	2,975	2,603	2,314	2,082	1,893	1,735	1,602	1,487	1,388
8 4,532	3,884	3.396	3,020	2,720	2,472	2,264	2,092	1,940	1,812
9 5,733	4,914	4,302	3,825	3,438	3,123	2,862	2,646	2,457	2,295
10 7,083	6,071	5,312	4,722	4,250	3,863	3,541	3,269	3,035	2,833
11 8,570	7,346	6,428	5,714	5,142	4,675	4,285	3,955	3,673	3,428
12 10,192	8,736	7,648	6,796	6,120	5,560	5,096	4,704	4,368	4,076
13 11,971	10,260	8,978	7,980	7,182	6,529	5,985	5,525	5,130	4,788
14 13,883	11,900	10,412	9,255	8,330	7,573	6,941	6,408	5,950	5,553
15 15,937	13,660	11,952	10,624	9,562	8,692	7,967	7,355	6,829	6,374
16 18,128	15,536	13,584	12,080	10,889	9,888	9,056	8,368	7,760	7,248
17 20,500	17,500	15,353	13,647	12,282	11,166	10,235	9,447	8,773	8,188
18 22,932	19,656	17,208	15,700	13,752	12,492	11,448	10,584	9,828	9,180
19 25,404	21,800	19,053	16,935	15,242	13,857	12,702	11,725	10,887	10,161
20 28,332	24,284	21,248	18,888	17,000	15,452	14,164	13,076	12,140	11,332
21 31,230	26,770	23,428	20,825	18,742	17,036	15,618	14,417	13,387	12,495
22 34,500	29,300	25,712	22,855	20,570	18,700	17,141	15,823	14,693	13,713
23 37,600	32,000	28,103	24,980	22,482	20,439	18,735	17,286	16,059	14,988
24 40,768	34,944	30,592	27,184	24,480	22,240	20,384	18,816	17,492	16,304
25	37,700	33,203	29,514	26,562	24,148	22,135	20,432	18,973	17,708
26	40,900	35,912	31,922	28,730	26,118	23,941	22,100	20,521	19,153
27	44,000	38,728	34,425	30,982	28,166	25,819	23,832	22,130	20,655
28	47,300	41,650	37,022	33,320	30,290	27,766	25,630	23,800	22,213
29		44,678	39,714	35,742	32,493	29,785	27,494	25,530	23,828
30		47,808	42,498	38,250	34,767	31,869	29,421	27,315	25,497

This table is intended to show the greatest weight a beam of cast iron will bear in the middle of its length, when it is loaded with as much as it will bear, so as to recover its natural form when the load is removed. If a beam be loaded beyond that point, the equilibrium of its parts is destroyed, and it takes a permanent set. Also, in a beam so loaded beyond its strength, the deflexion becomes irregular, increasing very rapidly with the weight of the load.

The horizontal row of figures, along the top of the table, contains the lengths in feet; that is, the distances between the points of support.

The first column contains the depth in inches, the other columns contain the weights in pounds avoirdupois. The breadth of each beam is one inch, therefore the table shows the utmost weight a beam of one inch in breadth should have to bear; and a piece five inches in breadth will bear five times as much, and so of any other breadth.

The load shown by the table is the greatest a beam should ever sustain, and therefore, in calculating this load, ample allowance must be made for accidents, and the weight of the beam itself must be included.

A TABLE, *to show the weight or pressure a cilindrical pillar or column of cast iron will sustain, with safety, in hundred weights.*

Length or height.	2 feet.	4 feet.	6 feet.	8 feet.	10 feet.	12 feet.	14 feet.	16 feet.	18 feet.	20 feet.	22 feet.	24 feet.
Diam. Inches.	Weight in cwts.	Weight in cwts.	Weight in cwts.	Weight in cwts.	Weight in cwts.	Weight in cwts.	Weight in cwts.	Weight in cwts.	Weight in cwts.	Weight in cwts.	Weight in cwts.	Weight in cwts.
1	18	12	8	5	3	2	2	1	1	1		
$1\frac{1}{2}$	44	36	28	19	16	12	9	7	6	5	4	3
2	82	72	60	49	40	32	26	22	18	15	13	11
$2\frac{1}{2}$	129	119	105	91	77	65	55	47	40	34	29	25
3	188	178	163	145	128	111	97	84	73	64	56	49
$3\frac{1}{2}$	257	247	232	214	191	172	156	135	119	106	94	83
4	337	326	310	288	266	242	220	198	178	160	144	130
$4\frac{1}{2}$	429	418	400	379	354	327	301	275	251	229	208	189
5	530	522	501	479	452	427	394	365	337	310	285	262
6	616	607	592	573	550	525	497	469	440	413	386	360
7	1,040	1,032	1,013	989	959	924	887	848	808	765	725	686
8	1,344	1,333	1,315	1,289	1,259	1,224	1,185	1,142	1,097	1,052	1,005	959
9	1,727	1,716	1,697	1,672	1,640	1,603	1,561	1,515	1,467	1,416	1,364	1,311
10	2,133	2,122	2,130	2,077	2,045	2,007	1,964	1,916	1,865	1,811	1,755	1,697
11	2,580	2,570	2,550	2,520	2,490	2,450	2,410	2,380	2,230	2,250	2,190	2,130
12	3,074	3,050	3,040	3,020	2,970	2,930	2,900	2,830	2,780	2,730	2,670	2,600

This table shows by inspection, the weight or pressure a cilindrical pillar or column of cast iron will bear with safety. The pressure is expressed in cwts., and is computed on the supposition that the pillar is under the most unfavorable circumstances for resisting the stress, which happens, when, from settlements, imperfect fitting, or other causes, the direction of the stress is in the surface of the pillar.

The horizontal row of figures at the top of the table contains the lengths or heights of the pillars in feet. The first vertical column contains the diameter of the pillar in inches.

The other vertical columns of the table show the weight in cwts., which a cast iron pillar, of the height at the top of the column, and of the diameter at the side column, will support with safety. Consequently, of the height, the diameter, and the weight to be supported, any two being given, the other will be found by inspection.

TABLE *of the Force of Winds, formed from the Tables of Mr. Rouse and Dr. Lind, and compared with the Observations of Col. Beaufoy.*

Velocity in miles per hour.	A wind may be denominated when it does not exceed the velocity opposite to it.	Velocity per second.	Force on a square foot.
6·8	A gentle pleasant wind	10 feet	0·229 lbs.
13·6	A brisk gale	20 . . .	0·915 . . .
19·5	A very brisk gale	30 . . .	2·059 . . .
34·1	A high wind	50 . . .	5·718 . . .
47·7	A very high wind	70 . . .	11·207 . . .
54·5	A storm or tempest	80 . . .	14·638 . . .
68·2	A great storm	100 . . .	22·872 . . .
81·8	A hurricane	120 . . .	32·926 . . .
102·3	A violent hurricane, that tears up trees, overturns buildings, &c. . . . . }	150 . . .	51·426 . . .

Accurate observations on the variation and mean intensity of the force of winds would be very desirable both to the mechanician and meteorologist.

TABLE OF DATA, &c.

USEFUL IN VARIOUS CALCULATIONS;

ARRANGED ALPHABETICALLY.

THE DATA CORRESPOND TO THE MEAN TEMPERATURE AND PRESSURE OF THE ATMOSPHERE, DRY MATERIALS; AND THE TEMPERATURE IS MEASURED BY FAHRENHEIT'S SCALE.

Air. Specific gravity, 0·0012; weight of a cubic foot, 0·0753 lbs., or 527 grains; 13·3 cubic feet or 17 cylindric feet of air weigh 1 lb., it expands $\frac{1}{480}$, or ·00208 of its bulk at 32° by the addition of one degree of heat.

Ash. Specific gravity, 0·76; weight of a cubic foot, 47·5 lbs.; weight of a bar one foot long, and one inch square, 0·33 lbs.; will bear without permanent alteration a strain of 3,540 lbs. upon a square inch, and an extension of $\frac{1}{404}$ of its length.

Atmosphere. The pressure of the atmosphere is usually estimated at 30 inches of mercury, which is very nearly $14\frac{3}{4}$ lbs. upon a square inch, and equivalent to a column of water 34 feet high.

Beech. Specific gravity, 0·696; weight of a cubic foot, 45·3 lbs.; weight of a bar one foot long and one inch square, 0·315 lbs.; will bear without permanent alteration on a square inch, 2,360 lbs., and an extension of $\frac{1}{570}$ of its length.

Brass, cast. Specific gravity, 8·37; weight of a cubic foot, 523 lbs.; weight of a bar one foot long and one inch square, 3·63 lbs.; expands $\frac{1}{93800}$ of its length by one degree of heat; melts at 1,869°; cohesive force of a square inch, 18,000 lbs.; will bear on a square inch without permanent alteration, 6,700 lbs.; and an extension in length of $\frac{1}{1333}$.

Brick. Specific gravity, 1·841; weight of a cubic foot, 115 lbs.; absorbs $\frac{1}{15}$ of its weight of water; cohesive force of a square inch, 275 lbs.; is crushed by a force of 562 lbs. on a square inch.

Bridges. When a bridge is covered with people, it is about equivalent to a load of 120 lbs. on a superficial foot; and this may be esteemed the greatest possible extraneous load, that can be collected on a bridge; while one incapable of supporting this load cannot be deemed safe.

Cast iron. Specific gravity, 7·207; weight of a cubic foot, 450 lbs.; a bar one foot long and one inch square, weighs 3·2 lbs. nearly; it expands $\frac{1}{162000}$ of its length by one degree of heat; greatest change of length in the shade in

18

this climate, $\frac{1}{1723}$; greatest change of length exposed to the sun's rays, $\frac{1}{1270}$; melts at 3,479°; and shrinks in cooling from $\frac{1}{98}$ to $\frac{1}{85}$ of its length; is crushed by a force of 93,000 lbs. upon a square inch; will bear without permanent alteration 15,300 lbs. upon a square inch, and an extension of $\frac{1}{1201}$ of its length.

Coal, Newcastle. Specific gravity, 1·269; weight of a cubic foot, 79·31 lbs. A London chaldron of 36 bushels, weighs about 28 cwt., whence a bushel is 87 lbs., (but is usually rated at 84 lbs.) A Newcastle chaldron, 53 cwt.

Copper. Specific gravity, 8·75; weight of a cubic foot, 549 lbs.; weight of a bar one foot long and one inch square, 3·81 lbs., expands in length by one degree of heat, $\frac{1}{103900}$; melts at 2,548°; cohesive force of a square inch, when hammered, 33,000 lbs.

Earth, common. Specific gravity, 1·52 to 2·00; weight of a cubic foot, from 95 to 125 lbs.

Elm. Specific gravity, 0·544; weight of a cubic foot, 34 lbs.; weight of a bar one foot long and one inch square, 0·236 lbs.; will bear on a square inch without permanent alteration, 3,240 lbs.

Granite, Aberdeen. Specific gravity, 2·625; weight of a cubic foot, 164 lbs., is crushed by a force of 10,910 lbs. upon a square inch.

Gravel. Weight of a cubic foot, about 120 lbs.

Gun Metal, cast, (copper 8 parts, tin 1.) Specific gravity, 8·153; weight of a cubic foot, 509$\frac{1}{2}$ lbs.; weight of a bar one foot long and one inch square, 3·54 lbs.; expands in length by 1° of heat, $\frac{1}{99090}$; will bear on a square inch without permanent alteration, 10,060 lbs.

Horse. Of average power, produces the greatest effect in drawing a load when exerting a force of 187$\frac{1}{2}$ lbs. with a velocity of 2$\frac{1}{2}$ feet per second, working eight hours in a day. A good horse can exert a force of 480 lbs. for a short time. In calculating the strength for horse machinery, the horse's power should be considered 400 lbs.

Iron, malleable. Specific gravity, 7·6; weight of a cubic foot, 475 lbs.; weight of a bar one foot long and one inch square, 3·3 lbs.; ditto,

when hammered, 3·4 lbs.; expands in length, by 1° of heat, $\frac{1}{143000}$; good English iron will bear on a square inch without permanent alteration, 17,800 lbs.,[*] = 8 tons nearly, and an extension in length of $\frac{1}{1400}$.

Lead, cast. Specific gravity, 11·353; weight of a cubic foot, 709·5 lbs.; weight of a bar one foot long and one inch square, 4·94 lbs.; expands in length, by 1° of heat, $\frac{1}{62800}$; melts at 612°; will bear on a square inch without permanent alteration, 1,500 lbs., and an extension in length of $\frac{1}{180}$.

Mahogany, Honduras. Specific gravity, 0·56; weight of a cubic foot, 35 lbs.; weight of a bar one foot long and one inch square, 0·243 lbs.; will bear on a square inch without permanent alteration, 3,800 lbs., and an extension in length of $\frac{1}{420}$.

Man. A man of average power produces the greatest effect when exerting a force of 31$\frac{1}{4}$ lbs., with a velocity of 2 feet per second, for 10 hours in a day.[†] A strong man will raise and carry from 250 to 300 lbs.

Marble, white. Specific gravity, 2·706; weight of a cubic foot, 169 lbs.; weight of a bar one foot long and one inch square, 1·17 lbs.; cohesive force of a square inch, 1·811 lbs.

Oak, good English. Specific gravity, 0·83; weight of a cubic foot, 52 lbs.; weight of a bar one foot long and one inch square, 0·36 lbs.; will bear upon a square inch without permanent alteration, 3,960 lbs, and an extension in length of $\frac{1}{430}$.

Pine, American, yellow. Specific gravity, 0·46; weight of a cubic foot, 26$\frac{3}{4}$ lbs.; weight of a bar one foot long and one inch square, 0·186 lbs.; will bear on a square inch without permanent alteration, 3,900 lbs.; and an extension in length of $\frac{1}{414}$.

Roofs. Weight of a square foot of Welsh rag slating, 11$\frac{1}{4}$ lbs.; weight of a square foot of plain tiling, 16$\frac{1}{4}$ lbs.; greatest force of the wind upon a superficial foot of roofing may be estimated at 40 lbs.

---

[*] Equivalent to a height of 5,000 feet of the same matter.

[†] This is equivalent to half a cubic foot of water raised two feet per second: or one cubic foot of water one foot per second. See *Buchanan's Essays,* vol. ii. p. 165, second edition.

Slate, Welsh. Specific gravity, 2·752; weight of a cubic foot, 172 lbs.; weight of a bar one foot long and one inch square, 1·19 lbs.; cohesive force of a square inch, 11,500 lbs.; extension before fracture, $\frac{1}{1270}$.

Steam. Specific gravity at 212°, is to that of air at the mean temperature, as 0·472 is to 1; weight of a cubic foot, 249 grains; when not in contact with water, expands $\frac{1}{480}$ of its bulk by 1° of heat.

Steel. Specific gravity, 7·84; weight of a cubic foot, 490 lbs.; a bar one foot long and one inch square, weight 3·4 lbs.; it expands in length by 1° of heat, $\frac{1}{157200}$; tempered steel will bear without permanent alteration, 45,000 lbs.; cohesive force of a square inch, 130,000 lbs.

Stone, Portland. Specific gravity, 2·113; weight of a cubic foot, 132 lbs.; weight of a prism one inch square and one foot long, 0·92 lbs.; absorbs $\frac{1}{16}$ of its weight of water; is crushed by a force of 3,729 lbs. upon a square inch; cohesive force of a square inch, 857 lbs.; extends before fracture, $\frac{1}{1783}$ of its length.

Tin, cast. Specific gravity, 7·291; weight of a cubic foot, 455·7 lbs.; weight of a bar one foot long and one inch square, 3·165 lbs.; expands in length by 1° of heat, $\frac{1}{72510}$; melts at 442°; will bear upon a square inch without permanent alteration, 2,880 lbs., and an extension in length of $\frac{1}{1600}$.

Water, river. Specific gravity, 1·000; weight of a cubic foot, 62·5 lbs.; weight of a cubic inch, 252·525 grains; weight of a prism one foot long and one inch square, 0·434 lbs.; weight of an ale gallon of water, 10·2 lbs.; expands in bulk by 1° of heat, $\frac{1}{358}$;* expands in freezing $\frac{1}{17}$ of its bulk; and the expanding force of freezing water is about 35,000 lbs. upon a square inch.

Water, sea. Specific gravity, 1·0271; weight of a cubic foot, 64·2 lbs.

Water is 828 times the density of air of the temperature 60°, and barometer 30.

Whalebone. Specific gravity, 1·3; weight of a cubic foot, 81 lbs.; will bear a strain of 5,600 lbs. upon a square inch without permanent alteration; and an extension in length of $\frac{1}{116}$.

Wind. Greatest observed velocity, 159 feet per second; force of wind with that velocity, about 57$\frac{3}{4}$ lbs. on a square foot.†

Zinc, cast. Specific gravity, 7·028; weight of a cubic foot, 439$\frac{1}{4}$ lbs.; weight of a bar one inch square and one foot long, 3·05 lbs.; expands in length by 1° of heat, $\frac{1}{61200}$; melts at 648°; will bear on a square inch without permanent alteration, 5,700 lbs.

---

* Water has a state of maximum density, at or near 40°; which is considered an exception to the general law of expansion by heat; it is extremely improbable that there is any thing more than an apparent exception, most likely arising from water at low temperatures absorbing a considerable quantity of air, which has the effect of expanding it; and consequently of causing the apparent anomaly.

† See Table, page 68.

A

DICTIONARY OF TECHNICAL TERMS

USED BY

ARCHITECTS AND ARTIFICERS.

Abacus. The upper member of the capital of a column whereon the architrave rests. In the Corinthian order, its four sides are curved inwards in segments of circles on the plan, and are decorated in the centre with a flower or some other ornament.

Abutment. The solid part of a pier from which an arch immediately springs.

Acanthus. A plant called in English, bear's breach, representations of whose leaves are employed for decorating the Corinthian and Composite capitals.

The leaves of the acanthus are used on the bell of the capital, and distinguish the two rich orders from the three others.

Acroteria. The small pedestals placed on the extremities and apex of a pediment. They are usually without bases or plinths, and were originally intended to receive statues.

Alcove. The original and strict meaning of this word, which is derived from the Spanish alcoba, is confined to that part of a bed-chamber in which the bed stands, separated from the other parts of the room by columns or pilasters. The seats in gardens have however in this country been designated by this term.

Alto Relievo. See Relief.

Amphiprostylos. In ancient architecture, a temple with columns in the rear as well as in the front.

Amphitheatre. A double theatre, of an elliptical form on the plan, for the exhibition of the ancient gladiatorial fights and other shows. Its Arena or Pit, in which those exhibitions took place, was encompassed with seats rising above each other, and the exterior had the accommodation of porticos or arcades for the public.

Ancones. The consoles or ornaments cut on the key-stones of arches, or on the sides of door-cases. They are sometimes made use of to support busts or other figures.

Annulet. A small square moulding, which crowns or accompanies a larger. Also that fillet which separates the flutings of a column. It is sometimes called a List or Listella, which see.

Anta. (*Antæ*, plural.) A name given to a pilaster when attached to a wall. Vitruvius calls pilasters *parastatæ* when insulated. They are not usually diminished, and in all Greek examples their capitals are different from those of the columns they accompany.

Antefixa, in ancient architecture. The ornaments of lions' and other heads below the eaves of a temple, through channels in which, usually by the mouth, the water is carried from the eaves. By some this term is applied to the upright ornaments above the eaves, in ancient architecture, which hid the ends of the Harmi or joint tiles.

Antepagmenta. The architraves round doors.

Apophyge. That part of a column between the upper fillet of the base, and the cylindrical part of the shaft of the column, which is usually curved into it by a cavetto.

Aqueduct. An artificial canal for the conveyance of water, either above or under ground. The Roman aqueducts are mostly in the former predicament.

Aræostylos. That style of building in which the columns are distant four and sometimes five diameters from each other, but the former is the proportion to which the term is usually applied. This columnar arrangement is suited to the Tuscan order only.

Aræosystylos. That style of building in which four columns are used in the space of eight diameters and a half. The central intercolumniation being three diameters and a half, and the others on each side being only half a diameter, by which arrangement coupled columns are introduced.

Arch. A scientific arrangement of bricks, stones, or other materials in a curvilinear form, which by their mutual pressure and support, perform the office of a lintel, and carry superincumbent weights, the whole resting at its extremities upon the piers or abutments.

Architrave. The lower of the primary divisions of the entablature. It is placed immediately upon the abacus of the capital.

Arris. The line of concourse, edge or meeting of two surfaces.

Ashler, in masonry. A term used among artificers, by which they designate common freestones, as they come out of the quarry, of different lengths and thicknesses. Nine inches however is their thickness.

Ashlering, in carpentry. Quartering in garrets to which the laths are nailed, about two feet and a half or three feet high, perpendicular to the floor, and reaching up to the underside of the rafters.

Astragal. A small moulding, whose profile is semi-circular. It bears also the name of Talon or Tondino. The Astragal is often cut into representations of beads and berries, and is used in ornamented entablatures to separate the faces of the architrave.

Attic Base. See Base.

Attic Order. An order of low pilasters, generally placed over orders of columns or pilasters. It is improperly called an order, for the arrangement can scarcely admit of such an appellation.

Back of a Hip. The upper edge of the hip rafter, between the two sides of a hipped roof, formed to an angle so as to range with the rafters on each side of it.

Back of a Rafter. The upper side of it.

Back of a Slate. The upper side of it.

Backer, in slating. A narrow slate laid on the back of a broad square headed slate, where the slates begin to diminish in width.

Balcony. A projection from the surface of a wall, usually supported by consoles and surrounded by a balustrade or railing.

Baluster. A small pillar or pilaster, serving to support a rail, see Plate XXIII. Its form is of considerable variety in different examples. Some-

times it is round, at other times square; it is adorned with mouldings and other decorations according to the richness of the order it accompanies.

Balustrade. A connected series of several balusters, as on balconies, terraces, around altars, &c. See Plate XXIII.

Band. A term used to signify what is generally called a face or fascia. It more properly signifies a flat low square profiled member, without respect to its place.

Bandelet. A diminutive of the foregoing term, used to signify any narrow flat moulding. The tænia on the Doric architrave is called its bandelet.

Bar Iron. A long prismatic piece of iron, being a rectangular parallelopiped, so prepared from pig iron, as to be malleable for the use of the smith.

Base. The lower part of a column, moulded or plain, on which the shaft is placed. The word also signifies any support, but it is in decorative architecture mostly used in the above sense. The earliest columns, as those of the Grecian Doric, were without bases, standing immediately on the floor or pavement of the portico.

Basilica. A town or court hall, a cathedral, a palace, where kings administered justice.

Basso Relievo. See Relief.

Batten. A name given by workmen to a piece of board, from two to four inches broad, and about one inch thick, the length is rather considerable, but undefined.

Battening. Narrow Battens fixed to a wall to nail the laths to.

Batter. A term used by bricklayers, carpenters, &c. to signify a wall, piece of timber, or other material which does not stand upright, but inclines from you when you stand before it; but, when on the contrary, it leans towards you, they say of its inclination that it overhangs.

Bead. A moulding whose vertical section is semi-circular. Hence when the edge of any piece is in this form, it is said to be beaded.

Beam. An horizontal piece of timber used to resist a force, or weight, as a tie-beam, which acts as a string or chain, by its tension; as a straining-piece, which acts by compression.

Bearer. Any upright piece used by way of support to another.

Bed, in bricklaying and masonry. The horizontal surfaces on which the stones or bricks of walls lie in courses.

Bed of a Slate. The lower side.

Bed Mouldings. Those mouldings in all the orders between the corona and frieze.

Bevel. An instrument for taking angles. One side of a solid body is said to be beveled with respect to another, when the angle contained between those two sides is greater or less than a right angle.

Bird's Mouth. The interior angle or notch cut on the extremity of a piece of timber, so that it may be received on the edge of another piece as a rafter.

Blocking-course. The course of masonry or brickwork on the top of a cornice.

Bond, in bricklaying and masonry. That connection between bricks and stones formed by lapping them upon one another in carrying up the work, so as to form an inseparable mass of building, by preventing the vertical joints falling over each other.

Bond Stones. Stones running through the thickness of the wall at right angles to its face, in order to bind it together.

Bond Timber. Timber laid in walls to tie them together longitudinally while the work is setting.

Bossage, a French term. Any projection left rough on the face of a stone for the purposes of sculpture, which is usually the last thing finished.

Bottom Rail, in joinery. The lowest rail of a door.

Boxings. See Linings.

Brace, in carpentry. An inclined piece of timber, used in trussed partitions, or in framed roofs, in order to form a triangle, and thereby stiffen the framing. When a Brace is used by way of support to a rafter, it is called a Strut. Braces in partitions, and span roofs are, or always should be, disposed in pairs, and introduced in opposite directions.

Break. Any projection from the general surface of a building.

Breaking Joint. The arrangement of stones or bricks so as not to allow two joints to come immediately over each other.

Brick Trimmer. A brick arch abutting against the wooden trimmer under the slab of the fire-place, to prevent the communication of fire.

Bridge, in masonry. An edifice or structure, consisting of one, or more arches, raised for passing a road-way over a river, canal, &c.

Cabling. The filling up of the lower part of a fluting of a column, with a solid cylindrical piece. Flutings thus treated are said to be cabled.

Caisson. A name given to the sunk pannels of various geometrical forms symmetrically disposed in flat or vaulted ceilings, or in soffits.

Caisson, in bridge building. A chest or vessel in which the piers of a bridge are built, gradually sinking as the work advances, till its bottom comes in contact with the bed of the river, and then the sides are disengaged, being so constructed as to allow of their being thus detached without injury to its floor or bottom.

Camber, in carpentry. The convexity of a beam upon the upper surface, in order to prevent its becoming straight or concave by its own weight, or by the burden it may have to sustain.

Canted. Obtuse angled.

Cantilivers. Pieces of wood framed into the front and sides of a house to sustain the eaves and mouldings over them.

Capital. The head or uppermost member belonging to a column or pilaster.

Carpentry. The art of arranging the main timbers of an edifice.

Cartouch. The same as modillion, except that it is exclusively used to signify those blocks or modillions at the eaves of a house. See Modillion.

Caryatides. Figures of women, which serve instead of columns to support the entablature.

Casement. A term used to signify sashes hung on hinges.

Casting or *Warping,* in joinery. The bending of the surfaces of a piece of wood from their original position, caused either by the weight of their own substance, or by an unequal exposure to the weather, or by the ununiform texture of the wood.

Caulicolus. The volute or twist under the flower in the Corinthian Capital.

Cavetto. A hollow moulding whose profile is a quadrant of a circle.

Ceiling, in plastering. The uppermost, horizontal or curved surface of an apartment opposite to the floor, generally finished with plastered work.

Centering. The temporary woodwork on which an arch is constructed.

Cincture. A ring, list or fillet at the top and bottom of a column, serving to divide the shaft of the column from its capital and base.

Clamp, in joinery. A piece of wood fixed to the end of a board with a mortise and tenon, or with a groove and tongue, so that the fibres of the piece thus fixed, traverse those of the board, and thus prevent it from casting: the piece at the end is called a clamp, and the board is said to be clamped.

Coat. A thickness or covering of plaster or other work done at one time.

Cofferdam. A case or cases of piling without a floor, in which the piers of a bridge are built.

Coffers. The sunk panels which are placed in vaults and domes, often ornamented with flowers in their centres.

Collar Beam. A beam framed crosswise betwixt two principal rafters above the plates on which they pitch.

Column. A member in architecture, whose vertical section through the axis is generally a frustum of an elongated parabola. Its plan is circular, and it consists of a base, a shaft or body, and a capital. It differs from the pilaster, which is square on the plan.

Composite Order. One of the orders of architecture.

Conge. Another name for the echinus or quarter round.

Console. See Ancones.

Corinthian Order. One of the orders of architecture.

Cornice. The projection, consisting of several members, which crowns or finishes the superior part of an entablature, or of any other part to which it is attached.

Corona. The flat square and massy member of a cornice, whose situation is between the cymatium above, and the bed moulding below; its use is to carry the water from the building.

Corridor. A gallery or open communication to the different apartments of a house.

Corsa. The name given by Vitruvius to any platband or square fascia, whose height is more than its projecture.

Coupled Columns. See Aræosystylos.

Course, in bricklaying and masonry. A continued level range of stones or bricks, of the same height throughout the whole length of the building as far as the solid part continues, uninterrupted by any aperture.

Course, in slating and shingling. An horizontal tier of slates or shingles.

Cradling. The timber ribs in arched ceilings and coves to which the laths are nailed.

Crown, in architecture. The uppermost member of the cornice called also Corona and Larmier.

Crown, or *King Post,* in carpentry. The post which in roofs stands vertically in the middle between the two principal rafters.

Cupola. A small room either circular or polygonal, standing on the top of a dome. By some it is called a Lantern.

Curtail Step. The lower step in a flight of stairs ending at its outer extremity in a scroll.

Cyma, called also *Cymatium,* its name arising from its resemblance to a wave. A moulding which is hollow in its upper part and swelling below. Of this moulding, there are two sorts, the Cyma Recta, just described, and the Cyma Reversa, whose upper part swells, whilst the lowest part is hollow.

Dado, in architecture. The die, or that part in the middle of the pedestal of a column, which is between its base and cornice. It is of a cubic form, and thence takes the name of Die.

Decastylos. A building having ten columns in front.

Dentils. Small square blocks or projections used in the bed mouldings of the cornices in the Ionic, Corinthian, and Composite Orders.

Diastylos. That style in which the intercolumniation or space between the columns consists of three diameters, some say four diameters.

Die or *Dye.* A naked square cube. Thus the body of a pedestal or that part between its base and its cap, is called the die of the pedestal.

Diminution. The gradual decrease of thickness towards the upper part of a column.

Dipteral. A term used by the ancients to signify a temple which had a double range of columns on each of its flanks.

Discharge. A term used to signify the relief afforded to any part on which a weight is to be borne. Thus, *Discharging Arches* are those used in the wall over a lintel to relieve the lintel of the weight which would be otherwise incumbent thereon.

Ditriglyph. An intercolumniation above which two triglyphs are disposed.

Dodecastylos. A building having twelve columns in front.

Dome. The spherical or other formed concave ceiling over a circular or polygonal building. Diminished Domes are those which are segmental on their section. Surmounted Domes are those which are higher than the radius of the base.

Door Frame. The surrounding case, into and out of which the door shuts and opens. It consists of two upright pieces and a head, generally fixed together by mortices and tenons, and wrought, rebated and beaded.

Doric Order. One of the five orders of architecture.

Dormer, in architecture. A window placed on the inclined plane of the roof of a house, or above the entablature, being raised upon the rafters, with its frame in a vertical position.

Dovetailing, in carpentry and joinery. The method of fastening boards, or other timbers together, by letting one piece into another in the form of the expanded tail of a dove.

Dragon Beams. Those horizontal pieces of timber on which the hip rafters pitch. They are framed into short diagonal pieces which tie the plates at the internal angles of a roof.

Dressings, in joinery. Any mouldings or other finishings.

Drift. The horizontal force of an arch, by which it endeavors to overset the piers.

Dripping Eaves. The lower edges of a roof, wherefrom the water drips on the ground.

Drops. See Guttæ.

Drum. The upright part of a cupola over a dome. Also the solid part or vase of the Corinthian and Composite capitals.

Eaves, in slating and shingling. The margin or lower part of the slating hanging over the wall, to throw the water off from the masonry or brickwork.

Echinus. The same as the ovolo or quarter round, but perhaps that moulding is only properly called echinus when carved with eggs and anchors, as they are termed. Echinus is the husk or shell of the chestnut, to which it is said to bear a resemblance.

Eggs. See Echinus.

Elbows. The sides or flanks of any panelled work.

Entablature. The assemblage of parts supported by the column. It consists of three parts, the architrave, frieze and cornice.

Epistylium. The same as Architrave, which see.

Eustylos. That intercolumniation, which, as its name would import, the ancients considered the most elegant, viz. two diameters and a quarter of the column. Vitruvius says this manner of arranging columns exceeds all others in strength, convenience, and beauty.

Exhedra. A recess in the ancient porticos or ambulatories for retirement from the crowd.

Extrados. The exterior or convex curve, forming the upper line of the arch stones: the term is opposed to the intrados or concave side.

Eye of a Dome. The aperture at its summit.

Eye of a Volute. The circle in its centre.

Façade. The face or front of any building towards a street, court, garden or other place, more usually however used to signify the principal front.

Facing. That part of any work which presents itself to the eye of the spectator.

Fascia. A flat member in the entablature or elsewhere, being in fact nothing more than a band or broad fillet. The architrave in the more elegant orders is divided into three bands: these are called fasciæ. The lower is called the first fascia, the middle one the second, and the upper one the third fascia.

Festoon. An ornament of carved work, representing a wreath or garland of flowers or leaves, or both interwoven with each other. It is thickest in the middle, and small at each extremity, where it is tied, a part often hanging down below the knot.

Fillet. The small square member which is placed above or below the various square or curved members in an order.

Fine Stuff, in plastering. A composition of lime slacked and sifted through a fine sieve, mixed with a proper quantity of hair, and sometimes a small portion of fine sand. Fine stuff is used in common ceilings and walls set to receive paper or color.

First Coat, in plastering of two coat work, is denominated 'laying' when on lath, and 'rendering' when on brick; in three coat work upon lath, it is denominated 'pricking up,' and upon brick, 'roughing in.'

Flashings. Pieces of lead let into the joints of a wall, so as to lap over gutters or other pieces.

Flatting. A coat of paint which, from the action of the turpentine used therein, leaves no gloss on the surface.

Floated Work. That which is pricked up, floated, that is, made of a perfectly plane surface by means of a tool called a float, and set, or roughed in floated and set.

Floated Lath and Plaster. Three coat work, the first whereof is pricking up, the second floating, and the third or setting coat of fine stuff.

Floating Skreeds, in plastering. Strips of plaster to float to; in cornices, wooden moulds edged with metal, are used for the execution of the work.

Floor, in architecture. The underside of the room, or that part whereon we walk. Floors are of several sorts, as of earth, of brick, stone, usually called pavement, and of wood.

Carpenters by the word *floor* understand as well the framed work of timber as the boarding over it.

Flue. The open concealed aperture of a chimney from the fire-place to the top of the shaft.

Flush. The continued surface in the same plane, of two contiguous masses.

Flutes or *Flutings.* The vertical channels on the shafts of columns, which are usually rounded above and below. They are sometimes circular or segmental, and sometimes elliptical on their horizontal section. In the Doric order they are twenty in number, in the other orders, the Tuscan excepted, which is never fluted, their number is usually twenty-four. They are occasionally cabled. See Cabling.

Footings. The spreading courses at the base or foundation of a wall.

Framing. The rough timber work of a house, including the flooring, roofing, partitioning, ceiling and beams thereof.

Fret or *Frette.* A kind of continued knot or ornament consisting of one or more small fillets running vertically and horizontally, and at equal distances in both directions. The sections of the channels below the surface of the fillet are rectangular.

Frieze or *Frize.* The middle member in the entablature of an order, which separates the architrave and cornice.

Frontispiece. The face or fore front of a house, but it is a term more usually applied to its decorated entrance.

Furniture. The external brass-work of locks, knobs of doors, and window-fastenings, &c.

Furring, in carpentry. The bringing a piece of sunk framing to a regular surface, by nailing thin pieces thereon.

Gable. The upright triangular piece of wall at each end of a roof from the eaves to the summit.

Guage, in plastering. A mixture of fine stuff and plaster, or putty and plaster, or coarse stuff and plaster, used in finishing the best ceilings, and for mouldings, and sometimes for setting walls.

Girder. The principal beam of a floor for supporting the binding joists.

Glyph. A vertical channel sunk on a tablet. Those of the Doric frieze are, from their number, called Triglyphs.

Groins. The lines formed at the intersection of two arches which cross each other.

Groove, in joinery. A term used to signify a sunk channel whose section is rectangular. It is usually employed on the edge of a moulding, stile or rail, &c. into which a tongue corresponding to its section, and in the substance of the wood to which it is joined, is inserted.

Ground Plate or *Sill.* The lowest plate of a wooden building for supporting the principal and other posts.

Grounds, in joinery. Pieces of wood, flush with the plastering to which the wooden finishings are attached.

Grout. Semi-liquid mortar.

Guilloche. An ornament composed of fillets in curvilinear directions, which form a continued series by their repetition.

Guttæ. Those frusta of cones in the Doric architrave, under the triglyph in the Doric order, which occur below the tænia. They are also found in the under part of the mutuli or modillions of that order. Sometimes they are, as in the Greek examples, a little curved inwards on their profile.

Hammer-beam. An horizontal piece of timber introduced towards the lower part of a rafter acting as a tie.

Harmus, in Greek architecture. The tile which covers the joint between two common tiles.

Headers, in bricklaying and masonry. Bricks or stones with the short face in front.

Heading Courses, in bricklaying and masonry. Those in which bricks and stones are laid entirely with headers.

Helix. The curling stalk under the flower in the Corinthian capital. See Caulicolus.

Hexastylos. A building having six columns in front.

Hips. The inclined pieces of timber at the angles of a roof; hence a hipped roof is that in which all the four sides have the same inclination to the horizon.

Holing, in slating. The piercing of the slates for nails.

Hypæthral. In the open air, or uncovered by a roof.

Hyperthyrum. The lintel of a doorway.

Hypotrachelion. The neck of a capital.

Jack Timbers, in carpentry. Timbers shorter than the whole length of other pieces in the same range.

Jambs. The side pieces of any opening in a

wall, which bear the piece that discharges the superincumbent weight of such wall.

Ichnography. The plan of a building.

Impages. Usually supposed to mean the rails of a door.

Impost. The capital of a pilaster supporting an arch. The impost varies in form according to the order with which it is used.

Inserted Column. One let into a wall.

Insulated. Detached from another building. A church is insulated, when not contiguous to any other edifice. A column is said to be insulated, when standing free from the wall; thus the columns of peripteral temples were insulated.

Intercolumniation. The distance between two columns.

Intertie, in carpentry. A horizontal piece of timber framed between two posts, in order to tie them together.

Intrados of an arch. The interior or concave curve of the arch stones.

Inverted Arches. Those whose key stone or brick is the lowest in the arch.

Joggle Piece. A truss post, with shoulders and sockets for receiving the lower ends of the struts.

Joggled Joints. Joints of stones or other masses, so indented as to prevent the one from being pushed away from the other by a force perpendicular to the pressures by which they hold together.

Joinery. The art of framing wood for the finishing of houses.

Joists. Those timbers in a floor which support, or are necessary to the support of the boarding or ceiling.

Ionic Order. One of the orders of architecture.

Key, in joinery. A piece of wood inserted into the back of another, whose grain runs in a contrary direction, to prevent the latter from warping.

Key Stone. That stone in an arch, which is equally distant from its springing extremities.

King Post. The middle post of a trussed piece of framing for supporting the tie beam at the middle and the lower ends of the struts.

Knee. A piece of timber naturally or artificially bent to receive another to relieve a weight or strain.

Lacunar. The same as Soffit, which see. It is however to be observed, that it is a lacunar only when consisting of compartments sunk or hollowed, without the separation of platbands or spaces between the panels. When they are added, it is called laquear.

Lantern. A square, circular, or polygonal erection on the top of a dome or other apartment to give light. See Cupola.

Larmier. Called also Corona, which see.

Lath. A slip of wood used in slating, tiling and plastering.

Lime and Hair, in plastering. A mixture of lime and hair used in first coating and floating. It is sometimes denominated coarse stuff: in floating more hair is used than in first coating.

Leanto. A building against another, in which the rafters of the former lean against the latter.

Leaves. Ornaments representing natural leaves. The ancients used two sorts of leaves, natural and imaginary. The natural were those of the laurel, palm, acanthus and olive, but they took such liberties in the form of these that they may almost be said to have been imaginary too.

Ledgers. Horizontal pieces of timber in scaffolding parallel to the wall opposite to which they are erected.

Lining, in joinery. The covering of an interior surface. Thus the linings or boxings of window shutters are the pieces which form the backs of the recesses into which the shutters fold. In a door they are the facings on the sides of the aperture. To a sash frame they are the vertical pieces parallel to the surface of the walls.

Lintel. A piece of timber or stone placed horizontally over a door, window, or other opening.

List, or *Listel.* The same as fillet or annulet.

Listing, in carpentry and joinery. The operation of cutting away the sap from the edge or edges of a board.

Luffer Boarding. Inclined boards placed above one another in an aperture, so as to admit air without permitting the rain to penetrate.

Luthern. The same as Dormer, which see.

Mantel. The horizontal cross-piece placed on the jamb of a chimney.

Meros. The plain part of a triglyph. That part between the channels.

Metoche. The space between two dentils.

Metopa. The square space between two triglyphs of the Doric order.

Mezzanine. A low story introduced between two principal stories.

Middle Rail, in joinery. That rail of a door which is level with the hand. The lock of the door is generally fixed on this rail.

Minute. The sixtieth part of the diameter of a column. It is the sub-division by which architects measure the smaller parts of an order.

Mitre. The diagonal junction of two pieces of wood, stone, etc.

Modillion. An ornament in the entablature of the richer orders, resembling a bracket. Modillions are placed, with the intervention of one or two small horizontal members, under the corona. They should be so distributed that their centres may always stand over the centres of the columns. In the Corinthian order they are enriched with carving; in the Ionic and Composite they are generally more simple. The term Mutulus, which is confined to the Doric order, is in fact the same as Modillion.

Module. A measure signifying the semi-diameter of a column. This term is only properly used when speaking of the Doric order. As a semi-diameter, it consists of only thirty minutes.

Monotriglyph. The arrangement in which only one triglyph is placed over an intercolumniation.

Mortise, in carpentry. A species of joint, wherein a hole or incision of a certain depth is made in the thickness of a piece of wood, for the reception of another piece called a tenon.

Mosaic Work. An assemblage of small pieces of pebbles, pieces of glass of various colors, or other pieces of materials, cut square and laid on a species of stucco, to form pavements, representations of pictures on walls, etc.

Mouldings. Those parts of an order which are shaped into various curved or square forms.

Mullion, or *Munnion,* in architecture. The short upright post or bar which divides any two lights in a window frame.

Mutulus. See Modillion.

Naked. The unornamented plain surface of a wall, column or other part of a building.

Naked Flooring, in carpentry. The timber work of a floor for supporting the boarding or ceiling or both.

Naos, or *Cella.* The part of a temple within the walls. That part of the temple in front of the Naos was called the Pronaos; and that in the rear the Posticum. This is the etymon of our English word nave.

Neck of a Capital. The space between the astragal above the shaft, and the annulet thereover.

Newel. The solid, or imaginary solid when the stairs are open in the centre, round which the steps are turned about.

Niche. A square or cylindrical cavity in a wall or other solid, generally for the reception of a statue.

Nosings of Steps. The rounded projecting edges of the treads or covers of the steps.

Notch Board. The board in a staircase notched or grooved out to receive the ends of the steps.

Nut, of a screw. A piece of iron pierced with a cylindrical hollow, whose circumference contains a spiral groove. The internal spiral of the nut is adapted to an external cylindrical spiral on the end of a bolt.

Obelisk. A tall slender frustum of a pyramid, usually placed on a pedestal. The difference between an obelisk and a pyramid, independent of the former being only a portion of the latter, is, that it always has a small base in proportion to its height.

Octastylos. A building with eight columns in its front.

Odeum. In ancient architecture, a place appropriated to the performance of music.

Œcus. In ancient architecture, an apartment adjoining to a dining-room.

Offset. The upper surface of the lower part of a wall left, by reducing the thickness of the super-incumbent part on one side or the other, or both.

Ogee, or *Ogive.* The same as Cyma, which see.

Opisthodomus. The enclosed space in the rear of a temple.

Order. An assemblage of parts, consisting of a base, shaft, capital, architrave, frieze and cornice, whose several services requiring some distinction in strength, have been contrived or designed in five several species, Tuscan, Doric, Ionic, Corinthian, and Composite: each of these has its ornaments, as well as general fabric, proportioned to its strength and use. These are the five orders of architecture, the proper understanding and application of which, constitute the foundation of all excellence in the art.

Orlo. The plinth of the base of a column or pedestal.

Orthography. A geometrical representation of the elevation or section of a building.

Ovolo. A moulding sometimes called the quarter round, from its profile being the quadrant of a circle; when sculptured it is called an Echinus, which see.

Palæstra, in Grecian architecture. A building appropriated to the purposes of wrestling, running, etc.

Panel or *Pannel*, in joinery, etc. A tympanum or square piece of thin wood sometimes carved, framed or grooved into a larger piece between two montants or upright pieces, and two traverses or cross pieces.

Parapet. From the Italian *Parapetto*, breast high. The defence round a terrace or roof of a building.

Parastatæ. Pilasters standing insulated. See Anta.

Parget. The plastering used in coating the internal surfaces of chimnies.

Party Walls. The brick or stone division between buildings in separate occupations.

Patera. The representation of a cup in bas relief, used as an ornament in friezes, fasciæ, and imposts.

Pavillon. In old French architecture, the projecting apartment at the flanks of a building.

Pedestal. The substruction under a column or wall. A pedestal under a column consists of three parts, the base, the die, and the cornice.

Pediment. The low triangular crowning ornament of the front of a building, or of a door, window or niche. Pediments are however sometimes in the form of the segment of a circle when applied to doors and windows. The pediment of a building is not unfrequently ornamented with sculpture.

Peridrome. The space, in ancient architecture, between the columns and the wall.

Peripteral. A term used by the ancients to signify a building encompassed by columns, forming as it were an aisle round the building.

Piazza. A square open space surrounded by buildings. This term is ignorantly used to denote a walk under an arcade.

Pier. A solid between the doors or windows of a building. The square or other formed mass or post to which a gate is hung. The solid support from which an arch springs. In a bridge, the pier next the shore is usually called an abutment pier.

Pig Iron. Short thick bars of iron, as they come from the smelting furnace.

Pilaster. A square pillar engaged in a wall.

Piles, in building, are large timbers driven into the earth to make a foundation to build upon in marshy ground.

Pillar. A column of irregular form, always disengaged and always deviating from the propor-

tions of the orders, whence the distinction between a pillar and a column.

Pitch of a Roof. The inclination which the sloping sides make with the plane, or level of the wall plate; or the proportion which results from dividing the span by the height. Thus, if it be asked what is the pitch of any given roof, the answer is, one-fourth, one-third, or one-half: when the pitch is one-half, the roof is a square, which is the highest that is used, or that is necessary in practice.

Planceer. The same as Soffit, which see.

Plaster. The material with which ornaments are cast, and with which the fine stuff of gauge for mouldings and other parts is mixed.

Platband. A square moulding whose projection is less than its height or breadth. The fillets between the flutes of columns are improperly called Platbands. The lintel of a door or window is sometimes called by this name.

Plate, in carpentry. A horizontal piece of timber in a wall, generally flush with the inside face thereof, for the reception of the ends of beams, joists or rafters.

Plinth. The square solid under the base of a column, pedestal or wall.

Portico. A place wherein persons may walk under shelter, sometimes raised with arches in the manner of a gallery. The portico is occasionally vaulted, but has frequently a flat soffit or ceiling. This word is also used to denote the projection before a church or temple, supported by columns.

Posticum. The back door of a temple, also the portico behind the temple. See Naos.

Posts. All upright or vertical pieces of timber whatever, as truss-posts, door-posts, quarters in partitions, etc.

Prick Posts. Intermediate posts in a wooden building, framed between principal posts.

Principal. Any main timber in an arrangement of carpentry.

Profile. The contour of the different parts of an order.

Propylæum, in Grecian architecture. A portico placed in front of gates.

Proscenium. That part of the stage of a theatre before the drop scene. In the ancient theatres it comprised the whole of the stage.

Prostylos. A building or temple with columns in front only.

Pseudodipteral. A term used by the ancients to signify a building or temple, in which the distance from each side of the cell to the surrounding columns, was equal to two intercolumniations, but wherein the intermediate range of columns which would occur between the outer range and the cell was omitted.

Purlines, in building. Those pieces of timber that lie on the principal rafters, to prevent the common rafters from sinking in the middle of their length.

Putlogs. Short pieces of timber at right angles to the walls used in making scaffolds.

Putty. A very fine cement made of lime only. It is thus prepared : dissolve in a small quantity of water, as two or three gallons, an equal quantity of fresh lime, constantly stirring it with a stick until the lime be entirely slaked, and the whole becomes of the consistency of mud ; so that when the stick is taken out of it, it will but just drop therefrom ; this being sifted or run through a hair sieve, to take out the gross parts of the lime, it is fit for use. Putty differs from fine stuff in the manner of preparing it, and in its being used without hair.

Pycnostylos. An intercolumniation equal to one diameter and a half.

Pyramid. A solid with a square, polygonal, or triangular base, terminating in a point at top.

Quarter Round. See Ovolo and Echinus.

Quirked Mouldings. Those which are suddenly convex, generally in one of the forms of a conic section.

Quoins. The external and internal angles of buildings or of their members : the corners.

Rafters, in carpentry. All the inclined timbers in the sides of a roof; as principal rafters, hip rafters, and common rafters.

Rail, in joinery. A horizontal piece which receives the tenons in a piece of framing, and into which the upper and lower edges of the panels are inserted.

Raising Plate, or *Top Plate.* That plate on which the roof is raised, or immediately placed.

Ramp. A concave bend in the capping of any piece of workmanship. Thus in stairs it is that concavity which occurs over risers or over a half or quarter space by the sudden rise of the steps.

Rebate, in joinery. A groove, channel, or recess, sunk on the edge of a board.

Recess. A part whose surface is within the general surface of the work.

Relief. The projection which a figure or ornament has, from the ground or plane on which it is sculptured. When the whole of the figure stands out, the work is said to be in Alto Relievo. When only half out, in Demi Relievo, and when it projects very little, in Basso Relievo.

Reticulated Work. That in which the courses are arranged in a form like the meshes of a net. The stones or bricks are square and placed lozenge-wise.

Ribs. Curviform timbers whereto the laths are nailed in an arched or coved plaster ceiling.

Ridge. The piece of wood against which the rafters pitch on the top of a house or other building.

Riser. The upright part of a step.

Roman Order. Another name for the Composite.

Rose. The representation of this flower is carved in the centre of each face of the abacus in the Corinthian capital, and is called the Rose of that capital. It is also used in decorating the caissons in the soffit of the corona, and in those of ceilings.

Rustic. The courses of stone or brick in which the work is jagged out into an irregular surface. Also work left rough without tooling.

Sag. The bending or curvature in the middle, which a horizontal piece of timber takes from its own gravity.

Salon. An apartment for state, or for the reception of paintings, and usually running up through two stories of the house. It may be square, oblong, polygonal or circular.

Sash. The frame work which holds the squares of glass in a window balanced by weights on each of its sides, hung thereto by lines running over pulleys at the top of the sash frame. When both the upper and lower sashes are moveable up and down, a sash is said to be double hung; when only one of them moves, they are said to be single hung.

Sash Frame. The wooden frame into which the sashes are fitted.

Scantling, in building. A measure, size or standard, whereby the dimensions, &c. of things are to be determined.

Scenography. The perspective representation of a building and its scenery.

Sciography. The doctrine of shadows.

Scotia. The name of a hollowed moulding, principally used between the tori in the bases of columns.

Shaft. That part of a column which is between the base and capital: it is also called the Fust as well as the Trunk of a column.

Shank. A name given to the insterstitial spaces between the channels of the triglyph in the Doric frieze. They are sometimes called the legs of the triglyph, and sometimes femora.

Shore. A piece of timber placed in an oblique direction for the security of a wall or other matter.

Sill. The horizontal piece at the bottom of any framing.

Skew Back, in brickwork and masonry. The sloping abutment for the arched head of a window.

Skirting. The narrow vertical board, standing on the floor round the sides of an apartment.

Sleepers. Pieces of timber on which the ground joists of a floor rest, or those laid under the planking in a bad foundation. The term was formerly applied to the valley rafters of a roof.

Socle. A square member of greater breadth than height, usually the same as plinth.

Soffit. The ceiling or under side of a member in an order. It also means the under side of the larmier or corona in a cornice ; also the under side of that part of the architrave which does not rest on the columns.

Spandrel. The space about the flanks or haunches of an arch or vault above the intrados.

Spars, in carpentry. The term by which the common rafters of a roof are known.

Springing. The lower part of an arch.

Stereobata, or *Stylobata.* The same as Pedestal.

Stiles. The vertical parts of any piece of framing or panelling.

Straight Arches. Heads of apertures which have a straight intrados in several pieces, with radiating joints, or bricks tapering downwards.

Straining Piece. A piece of timber for the purpose of preventing the nearer approach towards each other of two other pieces.

Stretchers. Bricks or stones laid lengthwise.

Stretching Courses, are those courses in which bricks or stones are laid lengthwise.

Struts. Pieces of timber which support the rafters, and which are supported by the truss posts.

Summer, in carpentry, is a large piece of timber which being supported on two stout piers or posts, serves as a lintel to a door, window, etc.

Surbase. The upper base of a room, or rather the cornice of the pedestal of the room, which serves to finish the dado, and to secure the plaster against accidents which might happen from the backs of chairs, or other furniture at an equal height.

Systylos. An intercolumniation equal to two diameters.

Tænia. The listel above the architrave in the entablature of the Doric order.

Talon. The same as Ogee.

Telamones. Figures of men that support an entablature.

Tenon, in carpentry. The end of a piece of wood diminished in its thickness, to be received into a hole in another piece called a mortise, for joining or fastening the two together.

Terminus. A stone anciently used to mark the boundary of property. A pedestal increasing upwards, or sometimes a parallelopiped for the reception of a bust.

Tetrastylos. A building having four columns in front.

Theatre. A building for the exhibition of dramatic shows. It was among the ancients semicircular in form, see Amphitheatre, encompassed with porticos, and furnished with numerous seats, which included a place called the Orchestra, in front of which was the floor of the theatre, called the Proscenium.

Thrust. See Drift.

Tie. A piece of timber placed in any position acting as a string or tie, to keep two masses together which have a tendency to spread to a more remote distance from each other.

Tongue. The projecting part on the edge of a board, which is inserted into a groove ploughed on the edge of another.

Toothing. Bricks projecting at the end of a wall, in order to bond thereinto a continuation of the wall when carried up.

Torus. A moulding of semi-circular profile used in the bases of columns.

Tread. The horizontal part of a step.

Triglyph. The ornament of the frieze in the Doric order, consisting of two whole, and two half channels, sunk triangularly on the plan.

Trimmers, in carpentry. Pieces of timber that are framed at right angles to the joists against the ways for chimneys, and well holes for stairs.

Trimming Joists, in carpentry. The two joists into which a trimmer is framed.

Trunk. See Shaft. When the word is applied to a pedestal, it signifies the dado, die, or body of the pedestal, answering to the shaft of the column.

Truss, in carpentry. A frame constructed of several pieces of timber, and divided into two or more triangles by oblique pieces, in order to prevent the possibility of its revolving round any of the angles of the frame.

Trussed Roof, in carpentry. One constructed within an exterior triangular frame, so as to support the principal rafters and the tie-beam at certain given points.

Tuscan. One of the orders of architecture.

Tympanum. The space enclosed by the cornice of the inclined sides of a pediment, and the horizontal fillet of the corona.

Valley. The internal angle formed by two inclined sides of a roof.

Valley Rafters. Those which are disposed in the internal angle of a roof to form the valleys.

Vase. A term sometimes used to denote the inverted bell-like form of the ground on which the leaves of the Corinthian capital are placed.

Vestibule. An anti-hall, lobby or porch.

Vault. An arched roof so contrived that the stones or other materials of which it is composed, support and keep each other in their places. Arched ceilings are a species of vaults, and are circular, elliptical or of other forms. When more than a semi-circle, they are called surmounted, and when less, surbased vaults.

Volute. The scroll which is appended to the capital of the Ionic order. There are volutes also in the Corinthian order, but they are smaller, more numerous, and always diagonally placed. In the Composite, the volutes are also diagonally placed, but larger than in the Corinthian order.

Voussoirs. The arch stones in the face or faces of an arch, the middle one is called the key-stone.

Wall-plates. The plates on which the joists and raising plates rest.

Water-table. A species of ledge left upon stone or brick walls, about eighteen or twenty inches or more from the ground, from which place the thickness of the wall is diminished.

Washer. A piece of flat iron with a hole, placed between the nut of a screw and the wood, to prevent the wood being gulled.

Weather Boarding. Feather-edged boards nailed upright with a lap over each other.

Wrought. Brought to a fair surface.

Zoophoros. The same as frieze.